The Complete
Tack Guide

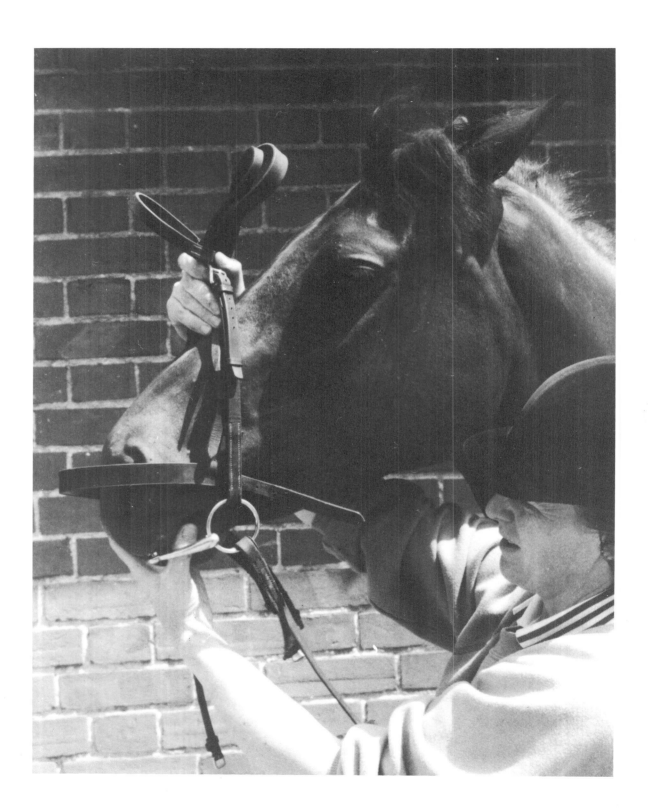

THE COMPLETE
Tack Guide

Vanessa Britton

The Crowood Press

First published in 1995 by
The Crowood Press Ltd
Ramsbury, Marlborough
Wiltshire SN8 2HR

British Library Cataloguing in Publication Data

A catalogue record for this book is available from the British Library

ISBN 1 85223 855 0

Photographs by Vanessa Britton.
Line-drawings by Jaqueline Darnell.

Typeset and designed by
D & N Publishing
DTP & Editorial Services
Crowood Lane, Ramsbury
Marlborough, Wiltshire SN8 2HR

Printed and bound by The Bath Press.

Dedication

For Derek, my most severe but fair critic, who is always right – at least 99% of the time!

Acknowledgements

My sincere thanks go to Wendy King, Maggie Davies and Susan Cox for their help with the photos, and to their horses for putting up with endless costume changes!

I am most grateful to the following individuals and companies for their help during the writing of this book: Vanessa Roberts, Thorowgood Saddlers; Debbie Murphy, Ireland Horsewear; Sheila Daking, Equetech; Peter Robinson, 3M; Tony Osborn, Mcleans Engineering; Bri-Tac; Eddie Palin Distribution; PI Associates; Roe Richardson, Francis and Drew Ltd; Sally Guiley, Classic Horse Clothing; K Harpley, Aerborn Equestrian Ltd; Clive Wetherall, Robinson Animal Healthcare; Susan Newell, FBS; Tracy Bird, Cottage Craft Industries; HEI Limited; Theresa Spencer, Fieldsafe; Griffin Products; Gary Daynes, Tirus Equestrian Products; Paul Brooker, Buxactic Ltd; Bridget Jennings and Liz Higgins, BJP; Robert Ellis, Koolpack UK Ltd; Jean Kittermaster; Carol Allison, CA Marketing.

Contents

Introduction

Go in to any good saddlery shop and you will be amazed at the extensive range of equipment it is possible to buy for your horse. It is no longer simply a question of asking for a certain item, as there may be literally dozens of varieties and makes available. Ask for a rug and you will be offered hundreds to choose from; ask for a pair of protective leg boots and you may still be in the shop two hours later. In order to prevent yourself from wasting both your time and money on items which are really unsuitable for your requirements, you need to have a clear understanding of what it is you want before you walk through the door. This is not easy, however, as horse tack is a complex subject which is further complicated by modern developments.

Technology has moved in to the tack room and old traditional saddlery is being challenged by new models and innovative ideas. Every year new bits and items of tack appear on the shelves: many would have been better left at the design stage, but others do find lasting popularity among hardened professionals.

We often pay great attention to schooling and fitness, yet overlook the effects our choice of tack is having on our horse. Every item, from bits to boots, has to some degree a positive or negative effect on performance. If we therefore take the time to study the effects our choices are having on our horse, we should always be able to use tack that will enhance, rather than detract from his performance.

Every item of tack that you use has, to some degree, a positive or negative effect on your horse's performance.

1   Bridles ——————————————————

A bridle is a fundamental item of tack which enables you to control the direction and speed of your horse's movement. Although a bridle can be very simple or more complex, when used accurately even the most basic types can act on up to seven intricate points of control on your horse's head. These control points are highly sensitive pressure areas which trigger certain responses from the horse when pressure is applied. Depending on the bridle (and bit) used, you can employ some, or all, of these control points to enable you to achieve a high degree of communication with your horse. However, these points can also be abused if you are unaware of the results your actions will have on your horse's head. Unsympathetic or plain harsh riding will cause the horse to flee from the discomfort or pain he receives, bringing about such evasions as napping, bucking and even rearing. Ignorance is no defence, so if you want to ride seriously you should take the time to learn the consequences of your actions through the tack you use from the minute you take hold of the reins.

TACK TIP

If you are unsure whether you are using the right bridle, ask yourself: whether your horse is going well and behaving himself? If he is, your tack obviously suits him. If he is not, his tack might not be right for him, but first you should discount any physical problems such as a sore back or sharp teeth. Be guided by your horse and share any worries with an experienced instructor.

BRIDLE CONTROL POINTS

There are three external control points on the head: the nose, the poll and the chin groove; and four internal control points within the mouth: the tongue, the roof of the mouth, the lips and the bars.

The Nose
The nose receives pressure indirectly from the bit, or directly from the nosepiece of a bitless bridle. Pressure on the bit causes the horse to react in his jaw, which in turn causes the action of the noseband to take effect. Where direct pressure is applied, the horse is encouraged to

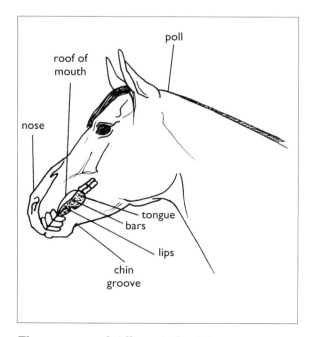

There are seven bridle control points.

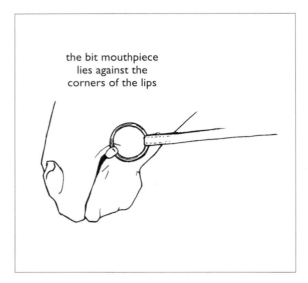

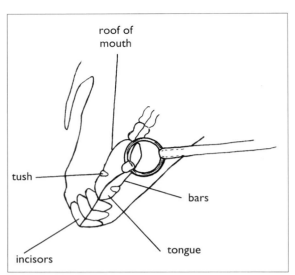

External view of the horse's mouth showing where the mouthpiece lies.

Internal view showing where the bit sits and how it may act upon the four internal control points.

tip his head inwards and, in the case of a bit-less bridle, to slow down. Direct pressure should only be applied to the solid nasal bone, not the soft cartilage around the nostrils.

The Poll

The poll, which lies directly behind the horse's ears, receives pressure indirectly from the bit, through the headpiece, resulting in a lowering of the head and neck.

The Chin Groove

The chin groove, or curb groove as it is known, receives pressure from the curb-chain which produces a downward and backward pressure, thus encouraging the horse to lower and tuck in his head. Nosebands which pass under the bit also have an effect on the curb groove.

The Tongue

How much pressure the tongue receives depends on whether it is coarse or fine. A coarse tongue will inhibit the bit from sitting on the bars of the mouth and so it will take the majority of the bit pressure. A neat tongue, with a sufficiently deep tongue groove, will allow the bit to sit correctly on the bars, and

thus minimal pressure will be taken by the tongue.

The Roof of the Mouth

Pressure is applied to the roof of the mouth by means of a high ported bit. However, such pressure is painful to the horse and so the roof is rarely used as a means of control in modern equitation.

The Lips

The corners of the lips receive pressure every time a contact is taken with a bit through the reins. While the horse is ridden with care, the corners of the mouth will remain sensitive and responsive to pressure, but harsh pulling on the reins will desensitize them, resulting in a 'hard-mouthed' horse. The head carriage of the horse and bit design will determine the direction of pressure.

The Bars

The bars are areas of toothless gum covering the lower jawbone between the incisor and molar teeth. All bits should sit on these bars with the degree of pressure being determined by the weight of the bit and the rider's hands.

A well-fitting snaffle bridle of the correct weight for this type of horse.

THE SNAFFLE BRIDLE

The term 'snaffle' bridle should not be taken literally as it does not mean that only a snaffle bit can be used. A better name to describe it would be 'single' bridle as the thing which determines a snaffle bridle is that only a single bit is used. There are various styles of snaffle bridle, some due to practical considerations, others simply a matter of personal taste. However, there are certain essential components whatever the style. The parts of a snaffle bridle are:

The Headpiece
The headpiece lies over the poll, to which the cheekpieces and browband are attached. Its purpose is to support the bit, by means of the cheekpieces, and to direct pressure on to the poll in response to the action of the bit.

The Throatlash
The throatlash does up just in front of the throat around the cheekbones. Once fitted it should allow a hand's breadth between it and the cheekbones. In many bridles it is permanently attached to the headpiece, but it need not be. Its purpose is to prevent the bridle from being pulled over the horse's head in the event of a fall.

The Browband
The browband slips up over the headpiece and sits in front of the horse's ears under his forelock. Its purpose is to prevent the bridle from slipping backwards. Once fitted it should admit one finger between it and the horse's head. Care needs to be taken that it is not too short as this will pull the headpiece tightly in to the base of the ears, causing sores. Conversely, if it is too long it is of little value as it will allow the headpiece to slip backwards.

The Cheekpieces
The cheekpieces hold the bit in the horse's mouth, supported by the headpiece. They enable the bit to be raised or lowered as desired. Cheekpieces of the correct size will do up around the middle holes of the headpiece. If they are too short they will only do up on the last hole or two, making them less secure. If they are too long they may have to do up on the top few holes of the headpiece, which could cause them to sit at the base of the ears interfering with the browband.

The Noseband
Nosebands come in various designs, the cavesson noseband being the most common. Each has its own fitting and use (*see* Chapter 2).

The Reins
The reins are the means of communication between the bit, or nosepiece of a bitless

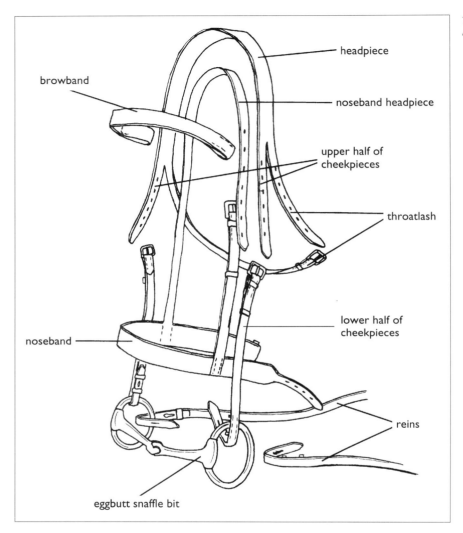

browband

headpiece

noseband headpiece

upper half of
cheekpieces

throatlash

lower half of
cheekpieces

noseband

reins

eggbutt snaffle bit

*The parts of a snaffle
bridle.*

bridle and your hands. There are various designs which are discussed further later in Chapter 2.

The Bit

To date, there are upwards of seventy snaffle bits listed, each with its own characteristics (*see* Chapter 3).

Fixing Methods

All of the various parts of the bridle need to be connected to each other in some way. Where a part provides adjustment it will fix to its connecting piece by means of a strap and buckle. Where an attachment is not adjustable, such as those components which fix to the bit, the reins and cheekpieces for example, there are various fixing modes. The *hook stud* fixing is the most common and the most practical for everyday use. Where you want a more streamlined look the item may be *stitched* on permanently. However, this does not allow the part to be removed for cleaning or substitution unless it is cut off. A simple *loop fixing* is quite effective, although not as secure as other methods because the stitched area is quite small. A loop is stitched on to the rein at one end and the other end of the rein is passed back through it. This type of fixing is commonly known as the 'monkey up a stick'. A *snap-billet* (similar to that found on some lead ropes) went out of fashion years ago, but has now been revived on many of the synthetic bridles. A simple *buckle fastening* completes the various fixing methods. This is strong, but is also bulky and therefore not suitable for showing or where the horse's appearance is of importance.

Snaffle Bridle Variations

The Dealer Bridle

This is designed to fit a multitude of horses where economy of time is of paramount importance. Instead of having a normal headpiece, the two cheekpieces are extra long and fasten together on top of the poll by way of a buckle and strap. As a dealer may show a great number of horses to one purchaser he cannot spend time fiddling about with separate bridles. He will put the dealer bridle on each horse in turn, taking but a few seconds to raise or lower the bit as appropriate.

The American Bridle

This bridle allows for very precise fitting. Instead of the headpiece and throatlash being attached, they are completely separate. The browband has two loops, one for the headpiece to pass through and one for the throatlash which has its own slip-head. The principle of one poll buckle is also often applied. This bridle is especially useful for a horse with a thick-set jaw, where the throatlash would not be in proportion with the cheekpieces.

The Rockwell Bridle

This bridle is designed to control the horse which pulls strongly. It has the noseband attached directly to the bit, by means of little figure-of-eight loops. The noseband is held in

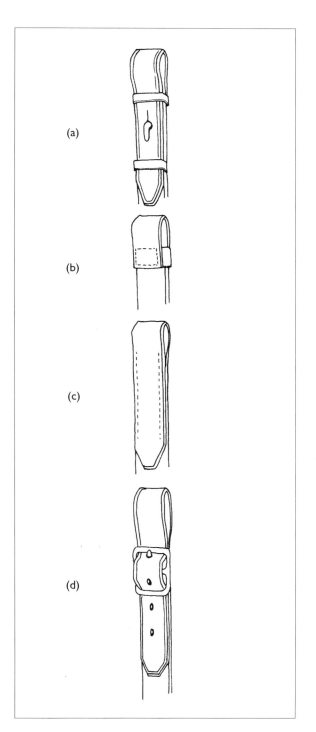

(a)

(b)

(c)

(d)

Fixing methods: (a) hook stud; (b) loop; (c) stitched; (d) buckle.

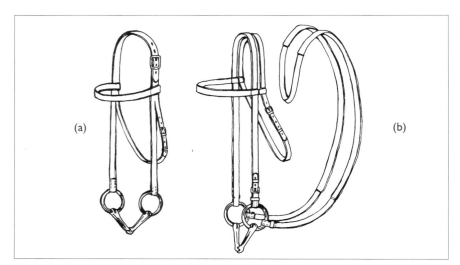

(a) Dealer bridle.
(b) American bridle.

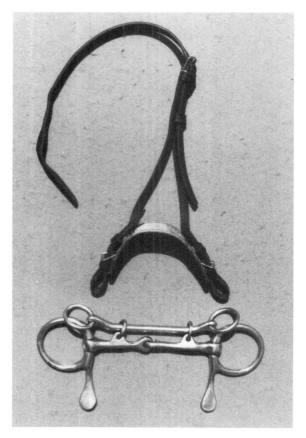

The Citation employs a noseband and bit in combination, which can exert extreme pressure on some of the bridle control points.

place by a strap which runs up the front of the horse's face and attaches to the headpiece at two points. It is used most often on horses who raise their heads and try to get their tongue over the bit, thus allowing them to pull away from their rider. If the horse tries this while wearing the Rockwell bridle, pressure on his nose will encourage him to lower his head, which allows the bit to act on the bars as it should.

The Citation

The Citation (aptly named after the American racehorse of that name who always wore one) or Norton Perfection as it is correctly known, is an even stronger variation of the Rockwell bridle. It still employs the noseband and bit in combination, but the bit is made up of two parts. The first is an ordinary spoon cheek jointed snaffle and to this is attached a very thin straight bar mouthpiece. The noseband is attached to the straight bar and the reins to the spoon cheek. The noseband is often made of strong elastic and, depending on how tightly it is fitted, the pressure exerted on the horse can be extreme. As this bridle is so strong, it should only be used by someone very experienced, who will be meticulous about fitting it and will use it correctly. For most horses there are far better alternatives.

THE DOUBLE BRIDLE

The double bridle is an awe-inspiring item of tack if you have never used one before and it takes time to understand its uses. Two bits are used – a curb and a bridoon – hence the prefix 'double', and their combined action needs to be appreciated before you can use one successfully. If used well, it can provide a high level of communication between you and your horse, but if used roughly it can cause your horse great pain. There is likely to come a time when you will need to use a double bridle, perhaps when showing or if advancing through the dressage levels, so it is better to get to grips with it sooner rather than later. Your horse will also have to become accustomed to its use, but providing he is going well in an ordinary snaffle and you introduce it slowly you should encounter few problems. Do not be afraid of using one through fear of hurting your horse as this will deprive you of a valuable means of communication with him. As long as you take it one step at a time and learn how to use one properly under supervision, you will soon find that the double bridle has some great attributes.

Assembly

While at first glance the double bridle looks like a complicated maze of bits, straps and buckles, it is really only an ordinary bridle to which you add another bit on its own slip-head and an additional pair of reins. One of the pairs of reins is slightly thinner than the other, to enable you to distinguish between the two without looking down when riding. Take a few minutes to study the pieces and you will soon be able to fit a double bridle together in seconds. To re-assemble a double bridle which has been completely dismantled, proceed as follows:

1   Firstly make up an ordinary bridle in the usual way.
2   Attach to this the curb bit to which the thinner reins are fixed.
3   Then attach the bridoon bit to its own slip-head and pass this up through the browband on the *near side* and fasten it on the *off side*.
4   Put on the bridle in same way as you would a snaffle but ensure that the bridoon lies immediately above the curb bit. To check this, make sure you can place two fingers between the mouthpiece of the curb and the

The double bridle is usual wear for showing ridden horses and it does add to the horse's appearance. Note how relaxed this horse seems to be.

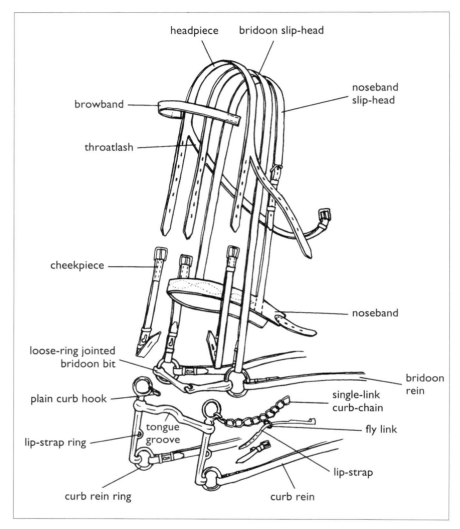

Parts of the double bridle.

headpiece

bridoon slip-head

noseband slip-head

browband

throatlash

cheekpiece

noseband

loose-ring jointed bridoon bit

bridoon rein

plain curb hook

single-link curb-chain

tongue groove

fly link

lip-strap ring

lip-strap

curb rein ring

curb rein

bit-ring of the bridoon. Adjust the noseband and throatlash as normal. The successful use of the double bridle relies on a clear knowledge of the action of the bits used. These are dealt with in detail in Chapter 3.

IN-HAND BRIDLES

As their name suggests, in-hand bridles are used for showing horses 'in-hand'. Such horses may be youngsters not yet ridden under saddle or they may be of a particular breed or type. The in-hand show bridle is used to complement the horse's looks. It usually has brass buckles and a neatly stitched noseband and browband. The noseband does not have its own slip-head, but instead runs through the cheekpieces. It is therefore vital to buy a bridle with cheekpieces of optimum length for your horse's head, otherwise the noseband will sit too high or low. A good type will allow adjustment at both the bit end and the headpiece end of the cheekpieces, thus allowing the bridle to be adjusted to suit the horse as he grows.

Some horses, such as hacks, have fancy browbands to make the horse look 'pretty'.

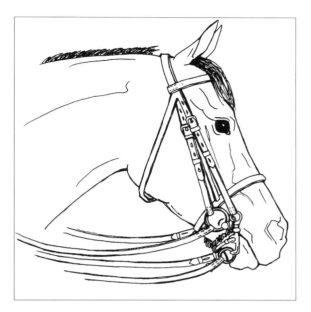

A double bridle fitted correctly.

When leading from an in-hand bridle it is customary to use either a plain leather lead line or a white webbing one. This is attached to the centre ring of a 'coupling' which is a small length of leather with a buckle at each end. These buckles attach to the bit rings on either side of the mouth, which facilitates leading from the centre of the bit, rather than just one side. On flighty youngsters it is often wise to put the lead line through the coupling ring and around the rear of the noseband. This will prevent the youngster from being jabbed in the mouth if he becomes excited and pulls or jumps around, thus averting him from developing a wariness of a bit in his mouth. Where a bit is simply fitted to improve appearance it is quite in order to lead just from the noseband.

A good type of in-hand bridle. It allows adjustment at both ends of the cheekpieces which ensures the noseband will lie in the correct place. Note the lead rein is fastened through the coupling and around the noseband.

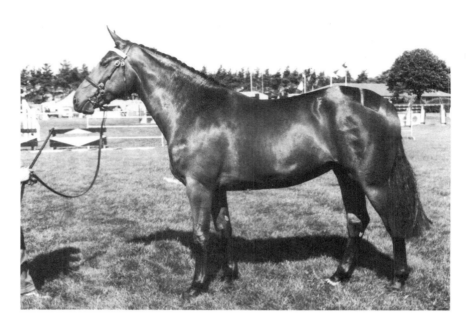

A white browband may be used to attract the judge's eye to a horse with no white markings.

BITLESS BRIDLES

There are no marks for guessing that a bitless bridle has no bit, but from there on the simplicity ends because there are various types and each has its own characteristics and use. Bitless bridles achieve control by applying pressure to the nose, chin groove and sometimes to the poll, in varying degrees depending on the individual design. However, they do rely on you being able to use your seat and leg aids properly, so if your horse does not respond to you when riding in one, this may be proof that your legs and seat are not as good as they ought to be. Conversely, if your horse works well from behind, it is proof that you do not rely on the bit to achieve a nice outline.

The bitless bridle has many applications. It can be used where a horse has a sore mouth, or a problem with his teeth which prevents use of a bit. It can be useful for a horse which has abnormal mouth conformation, or for a horse who through poor riding no longer responds well to bit pressure. In some cases, and for no apparent reason, a horse will not go well in any type of bit, but seems to prefer the action of a bitless bridle. While the bitless bridle does have sufficient stopping power, its one drawback is that it would be hard to perform lateral movements while using one.

Bitless bridles are very popular with endurance riders, because their horses can eat and drink *en route* without having to have their tack removed first. It must also be preferable for the horse not to have a bit in his mouth while undertaking many hours under saddle and undoubtedly the bitless bridle has prevented many sore mouths in this type of situation.

The Hackamore

The hackamore is a much misunderstood bridle. Many people refer to all bitless bridles as hackamores, when in fact it is only one type which belongs to the group of bitless bridles.

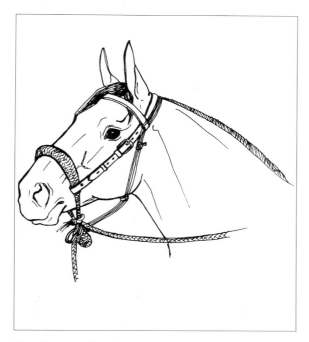

Bosal or true 'hackamore'.

However, names linger, so if you hear of a bridle being referred to as a hackamore do not automatically assume it is one, as it is more than likely to be a different type altogether.

The true hackamore is no more than a bosal, which is a padded noseband suspended on a headpiece, that usually has one ear slot. The padded noseband is usually made of plaited rawhide, which is jointed together under the chin by a heavy knot. The reins run from this knot to the rider's hands. In some variations a further strap (or two thin leather laces) runs from this knot to a throatlash which is separately attached through a browband. It is not used very much in the UK but does find favour with western riders in the USA and Canada, as the horse is controlled as much by body weight and neck-reining as by the action of the hackamore. Where direct pressure is applied to the noseband, the action is simply one of backwards pressure, which restrains the horse and also suggests to him that he lowers his head.

Blair's Pattern

This is the type of bitless bridle commonly associated with the name 'hackamore'. There are two designs, Blair's pattern 1 and Blair's pattern 2, the latter being the most common bitless bridle in use throughout Europe.

Blair's Pattern 1
The noseband is made up of four pieces: there is an adjustable padded nosepiece at the front which connects to a flat band of leather on each side of the horse's face, to which a rear, adjustable curb strap attaches. Suspended from these flat bands of leather are metal cheeks which run down below the horse's mouth ending in fixed rings to which the reins are attached. A half-moon metal bar attaches both cheekpieces together just above the rein rings, facing backward towards the horse's neck. This design employs a separate throatlash.

The longer the cheeks the more severe the action; some designs have cheeks of up to 30cm (12in) in length. The noseband is fitted slightly lower than a cavesson noseband (*see* page 25) which in no way interferes with the horse's breathing; however, this is adjusted up and down a hole at frequent intervals to prevent chafing and even calluses from forming. The curb-strap sits further up than a normal curb-chain, applying pressure half-way between the upper cheekbones and the curb groove.

This pattern achieves control by combining pressure on the nose with pressure on the curb groove. Leverage is obtained by applying more pressure on the reins and where this is considerable, poll pressure is also applied.

Blair's Pattern 2
This is similar in design to Blair's pattern 1, but is not as severe because the cheeks are much shorter and are directly attached to the noseband, headpiece and rear strap. It is often referred to as the 'English hackamore', supposedly because it is seen on many English

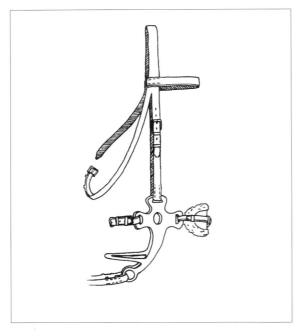

Types of bitless bridle: Blair's pattern 2.

The German bitless bridle, which has long shanks providing a large degree of leverage.

horses! The noseband needs to be secured fairly tightly in order to control the horse sufficiently well, though care must again be taken to ensure that it does not sit too low on the nose and thus restrict the horse's breathing. Both the noseband and curb-strap, or chain, need to be padded in order to prevent chafing. Control is achieved in the same way as Blair's pattern 1, although to a lesser degree.

The German Bitless Bridle

This is similar in action and severity to the Blair's pattern 1, but differs in design. It has a rolled, padded noseband, which is sometimes covered in sheepskin. It concentrates more pressure over a smaller area on the horse's nose and so can be very severe if great pressure is applied. The cheek shanks can be very long and so provide a large degree of leverage, which acts upon the poll when only the slightest contact is taken up on the reins. Care must obviously be taken with this type of bridle, but nevertheless in experienced hands it does enable a strong horse to be kept under control where a bit is not suitable.

WS Bitless Pelham

This allows a degree of precision which eludes other types of bitless bridle. As with an ordinary Pelham bit (*see* page 49), the WS can be used with two reins. One is similar to that of a snaffle rein, in that its action is direct, in this case on the nose of the horse. The other 'curb' rein employs leverage acting on the curb groove, nose and poll. The cheek shanks can also be used independently of each other which is obviously desirable where an element of accuracy is required.

The whole structure is made of metal, although the noseband is well padded. The cheeks are shorter than in the Blair's pattern 1, and have both curb-chain and lip-strap attached. Sometimes it is more desirable to use an elastic or leather curb-strap, especially where the horse resents the feel of the chain.

Types of bitless bridle: the WS Bitless Pelham.

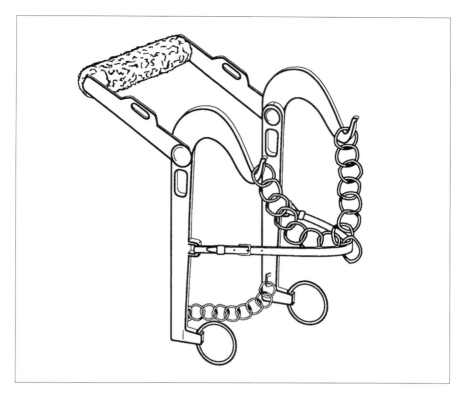

To look at, the WS is probably the most startling bitless bridle, but in practical terms its influence over the horse is closest to that obtained by the use of the double bridle.

Bitless Jumping Bridle

This is another pattern which often gets the name 'hackamore' applied to it, being commonly referred to as a jumping hackamore. Like the dealer bridle there is only one buckle for adjustment at the poll. The two long cheekpieces split into two branches midway down the horse's cheekbones, which attach either side of the head to two small fixing rings on a rolled, padded noseband. This noseband is open-ended, each end terminating in a ring to which the reins are attached. The back chinstrap attaches to the rear cheekpiece attaching ring on either side of the noseband.

This type of bridle is much simpler in action than those with cheek shanks as it creates no leverage and thus no poll pressure, and is useful when jumping as the horse is not going to overbend coming in to a fence. A contact with the reins simply puts pressure on the nose and lower jaw.

Scawbrig

This is the simplest type of bitless bridle currently in use. It is mild in action as it has no cheek shanks and therefore no leverage on the poll. It can be built up in three stages until a bit is also employed, so it is very useful when training a young horse or when retraining a spoilt older horse, to get them to accept bit pressure. In its simplest form the Scawbrig is no more than a noseband with reins. The padded nosepiece ends in two medium-sized rings, to which the cheekpieces are attached. A back strap then passes through these rings to form a chin-strap. This may also terminate in rings to which the reins are fitted, or it may

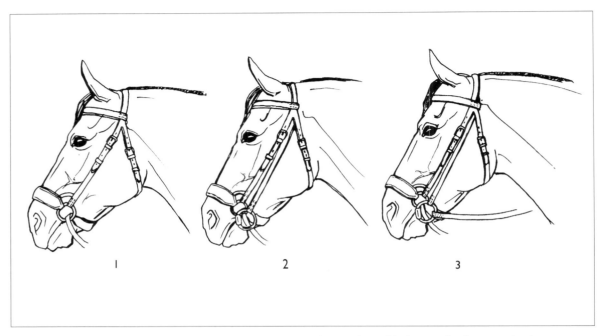

The Scawbrig, a simple type of bitless bridle which can have a bit added as and when required.

A synthetic Scawbrig. As contact is taken on the reins, pressure is applied directly to the nose.

extend into lengths of leather, thus forming the reins itself. This can be visualized as a dropped noseband without the chin-strap, which has an extra long rein passing in through the ring on the near side, around the lower jaw and out through the ring on the far side, forming the two reins.

As a contact is taken with the reins, so the the rear chin-strap tightens and pressure it placed on the front nosepiece and the lower jaw. During schooling, a bit may be added on its own slip-head, so that it is simply suspended in the mouth. No reins are attached, so no pressure is applied to the mouth. However, the horse does become accustomed to the feel of a bit, and a horse nervous of one will begin to realize that there is nothing to fear from it. Appropriate reins can then be added and you can then take up a contact with your horse's mouth as desired. However, this must be done gradually, if your horse is to stay fearless of a bit. Still ride off the noseband, taking weeks or even months until full control with the bit is achieved.

The restrainer bridle, used for leading or lungeing a very unruly horse.

The Restrainer Bridle

The restrainer bridle also has no bit and is used for leading or lungeing a very unruly horse. It has a metal noseband which is suspended on two cheekpieces. This noseband has a ring on the centre to which a lead rope is attached. While the horse behaves himself there is no action. If he decides to jump about or try to evade your requests on the lunge or when leading you simply hold firm and he will be putting pressure on his nose by pulling against the metal noseband. Horses dislike this intensely and soon learn to come under control. It has been used with good effect on horses who rear when being lead. If you pull on the horse's mouth when he rears by grabbing hold of the reins and tugging at the bit, he is likely to do it all the more to get away from you. The restrainer bridle seems to have the opposite effect in that the sensation of the metal ring on his nose makes him lower his head, thus relieving any pressure and so he comes back down to the ground.

Sometimes it is a good idea to pad the noseband with sheepskin to reduce the possibility of it digging into the skin if the horse becomes very unruly.

SYNTHETIC BRIDLES

The traditional material for bridles has always been leather, which may be plain, stitched, rolled or infilled with panels of various materials and designs. However, synthetic tack is becoming extremely popular as its benefits are numerous. It is easy to clean, as it can be put in the washing machine; easy to fit, as many designs have snap hooks instead of buckles so, once adjusted to an individual horse, it takes seconds to put on; highly versatile, as different pieces can be snapped on, or taken off at a moment's notice to change an ordinary bridle into a bitless one, or even into a headcollar (this is known as a *combination bridle*). Because of their versatility and quick and easy use, synthetic bridles find favour in many trekking centres and with many endurance riders. Where a horse is fresh at the start of a long-distance ride a bit can be used. As the horse settles down along the way the bit can be removed to facilitate feeding and to prevent mouth sores; and at the finish of the ride a couple of clips are removed, a lead rope attached and the horse has a headcollar to travel home in. The saving in time and

Bri-Tack's synthetic combination bridle, which can be changed into a Scawbrig or a headcollar, simply by unclipping a few pieces.

effort by the use of synthetic tack is catching on with busy horse owners who have not got time to spend cleaning tack, when there is a job to go to and a family to look after, as well as a horse to feed and groom.

> **TACK TIP**
>
> When buying synthetic tack do make sure you buy good-quality items. Those items of an inferior standard have been known to stretch with use, so a new pair of 130cm (50in) reins soon becomes a 150cm (60in) weaker pair!

HEADCOLLARS

The headcollar is an essential piece of equipment. Without it you cannot lead your horse, tie him up or generally handle him safely. There are various types of headcollar on the market, from those used for everyday wear to high-quality leather ones for show. Headcollars come in three standard sizes: pony, cob and full, although many are fully adjustable and will fit nearly any horse.

Nylon Webbing Headcollars
These are good everyday headcollars and are fully adjustable. They are strong and can be washed in the washing machine, which obviously saves time on cleaning and saddle soaping. However, these headcollars will not break in an emergency and should not, therefore, be left on in the field or in the stable. When tying up a horse wearing a nylon headcollar, tie the lead rope to a piece of breakable twine, so that in the event of an emergency it will snap. If you do need to leave a headcollar on in the field use a 'fieldsafe' headcollar.

Leather Headcollars
These always look nice and do offer a good grip on the horse's head. Their one drawback is that they are expensive because they are made of very thick leather which is usually stitched by hand. However, they are an excellent investment, as they will last a lifetime if cared for properly.

When you are buying a leather headcollar do not be tempted to go for a cheaper one as this will almost certainly be of an inferior standard. Select the type which has an adjustable noseband as well as a jowl strap. Non-adjustable nosebands are notoriously big – probably so that any horse can wear them – and they sag in time, which provides them the opportunity of slipping off the horse's nose if they are also a little too long. The ultimate leather headcollar is one that is made to measure. This will provide your

Arab showing headcollars are very light and may be highly decorated.

horse with a regularly used item of tack that will not rub or flop about on his nose. To establish a good fit the noseband should lie about 5cm (2in) down from the horse's cheekbones, when the cheekpiece is done up on the middle holes. You should be able to fit three fingers between the noseband and the horse's nose.

Showing Headcollars

These usually have brass fittings, and double-lined stitching to draw attention to the head. The brass square joiner attaching cheekpiece to noseband should be sufficiently wide to take a neat leather strap which enables a bit to be attached if required.

Arab horses are usually shown in a head-collar, but of a very unusual style. The Arab headcollar is very fine and light and may be highly decorated with inlaid plaited leather. However, this fine look should not be taken to the extreme of being nearly non-existent as this would pose a safety risk and could mean that the horse could break free if he put up a fight – which happens all too often in in-hand showing classes!

The 'Controller' Headcollar

This is an innovative model designed to control the more lively horse. Instead of the jowl strap fixing to the noseband, it is looped through a metal ring underneath the horse's jaw. At the end of the loop there is another ring to which the lead rope is attached. While the horse is behaving well the headcollar acts as any other. However, as soon as the horse snatches his head up or jumps about, the lead rope pulls on the loop, thus automatically tightening the headcollar. This puts pressure on the nose and poll which encourages the horse to bring his head down and therefore back under control. The beauty of this design is that the horse operates it himself, and you still have only one lead rope to worry about.

The Fieldsafe Headcollar

Whether or not to chance leaving a headcollar on the horse in the field is an ever-present problem. You may need to leave a headcollar on in the field for a variety of reasons, perhaps because your horse needs to wear a fly fringe,

The controller headcollar applies pressure to the poll and nose if the horse lifts his head up too far.

or is difficult to catch, but there is always the danger that it could become caught on a fence or a tree. The solution to this problem is the fieldsafe headcollar. It is made from soft cotton, with seams on the outside to avoid rubbing and has smooth rubber rings, which will break apart if your horse does get caught up. Fieldsafe headcollars are not meant for control, so it is advisable to use a conventional headcollar for leading your horse from the field once caught.

Halters

Halters are made of rope or webbing, and are an all-in-one design that can be adjusted to fit any size of horse. The headpiece is slipped up over the horse's ears, while the noseband is being drawn up the horse's face. The rope is pulled which tightens the noseband and it is then knotted to prevent the noseband from tightening should the horse pull on the lead rope. Because of its ability to fit any horse the halter is used extensively in dealing yards and studs, where many horses pass in and out.

Foaling Slips

A foaling slip (or foal-slip) is the name given to the foal's first headcollar. It is made of soft leather and is highly adjustable as the foal grows at a tremendous rate in the first weeks of his life. Its design is different from that of normal headcollars as its headpiece and noseband both run to a ring under the jaw. A diagonal strap across the foal's cheekbone stabilizes the construction. A small foal-slip may be made as an all-in-one design, fitting around the foal's face in a figure-of-eight arrangement, in which case the ring fits around the straps where they cross under the jaw. This ring has a 16cm (6in) strap sewn on to it which facilitates catching the foal without scaring him.

Lead Ropes

A lead rope is essential in order to tie up or lead the horse. They are made out of cotton, heavy jute or nylon. The nylon type is the least favourable as it can fray, is sometimes hard to secure a quick release knot with and will cause a nasty burn if pulled sharply through an ungloved hand. In order to attach the lead rope to the headcollar a clip is needed. These are made in various designs, but the snap hook is the most common. When attaching a lead rope to a headcollar always ensure the point of the snap hook faces the horse's neck. Ghastly accidents have happened where the point faces the horse's lip, including an incident where the horse grabbed the clip in his mouth and it went straight through his lip, splitting it open.

2 Bridle Accessories

Having provided the means of control over your horse by fitting a basic bridle, there may come a time when you want to communicate with him in a more refined way. To a certain extent your riding skills will convey these messages, to a greater or lesser degree depending on your level of skill. However, in order to help your horse understand further what you require, it may be necessary to change one sort of component for another type. Some bridle components, such as the cheekpieces for example, do no more than hold the structure together. Others, for instance the noseband, may assist you in directing pressure on one or more of the control points; while others, such as the reins, simply vary in how they feel for you, the rider, to handle.

TYPES OF NOSEBAND

Nosebands are used most often to assist and, in some cases, to alter the action of the bit and by doing so help to encourage the horse to accept it. Some are no more than a device for preventing the horse from opening his jaws, whereas others are more complex in design and action. It is evident that on many occasions a horse does not require the effect of a noseband, but that he wears one to improve his appearance. A white-faced horse will often wear a wide noseband to break up the large plain area, for instance.

Selecting the appropriate noseband for your horse is very important. Great thought needs to be given to your horse's way of going and to other tack being used. A noseband is only part of the bridling equation, and all items used together should complement each other. This is not a concept wholly understood by many riders, who often only see the individual effects of items; but what, for instance, is the point of using one item of tack to raise the horse's head, when another item asks him to lower it? Knowing the effect the noseband will have in relation to the bit and martingale also employed is a crucial part of achieving a good understanding with your horse. Remember, it is not only you who needs to understand the effect of the noseband, but your horse as well. If he gets conflicting messages from the tack he wears, what is he to think?

One of the myths of using nosebands is that they are used to clamp a horse's mouth shut. This is simply not the case. Generally they are used to prevent the horse from opening his mouth too wide and thus being able to cross his jaws and evade the action of the bit. If a horse's mouth is clamped shut he will be physically incapable of flexing his jaw and therefore will be prevented from accepting the bit as desired. Too many people use a certain type of noseband without giving any thought to its effects, simply because they think it looks fashionable, or happened to be the type on the bridle when they bought it. How would they like to be put in a straight-jacket because it was the latest fashion?

Cavesson

This is the simplest noseband in use today and often suits a horse for his entire life.

Construction
The cavesson is simply a band of thick leather,

The cavesson noseband is the most popular for all sorts of horses.

suspended on its own slip-head, which completely surrounds the horse's nose and fixes by means of a single buckle at the rear of his lower jaw. One that is well made will not sag, but will remain at right angles to the slip-head.

Fitting

The slip-head passes up through the browband on the off side of the horse's head, sitting over the horse's poll underneath the headpiece. It does up on the near side. The slip-head should be concealed by the bridle cheekpieces. If it protrudes in front of them, then the front length of the noseband is too short, which is a common design fault. When correctly fitted it should lie midway between the projecting cheekbone and the bit, which is usually about 10cm (4in) from the nostrils. It is tightened until it will admit two fingers between it and the horse's nose. It may be broad or fairly narrow depending on the horse's face.

Use

The cavesson is the only noseband used in conjunction with a double bridle. When used on hunters it is usually broad and plain, but when used on hacks and lighter horses it is narrow and often prettily stitched or rolled. Its only action is that of preventing the horse from opening and crossing his jaws and is largely used as an anchor point for a standing martingale. Horses ridden by novice riders should only wear a cavesson, as such riders will not understand the effects or correct use of more complicated designs. It is also the only noseband which should be used with a curb bit, as those nosebands which employ a lower chin-strap can interfere with the curb's action. Some top riders do ignore this principle and will use a curb bit with a lower strap noseband in various disciplines, but unless you have their skill and ability it is best not to copy them.

If you have a horse who does open his mouth and cross his jaws, but fights a noseband with a lower strap, you can use the cavesson two or so holes tighter than normal to discourage him from doing so.

Drop

The drop noseband seems to have fallen out of favour in recent years, although this is through no fault of horses themselves. It is not because horses do not go well in them, but because they do require an amount of precise riding to have the right effect, and therefore show up faults in one's riding ability.

Construction

The drop noseband differs from the cavesson in that the front and rear straps are separate. These join at a small ring suspended on the cheekpieces. A good make will have a spike projecting in to both the nosepiece and slip-head which prevents the nosepiece from sagging down over the nostrils, or a connecting half-moon strap running from the base of the slip-head to the back of the nosepiece which serves the same purpose. A very well made

The drop noseband does require a certain amount of precise riding in order to have the right effect.

ages the horse to lower his head which then permits the bit to apply more pressure on the bars, still indicating a downward and inward direction (a snaffle used alone produces an upward motion). It is therefore possible to achieve a slight degree of flexion with a snaffle bit and a drop noseband.

In situations where more control is needed the drop noseband is also a valuable aid. It will not allow the horse to open and cross his jaws, therefore he has to receive the action of the bit as it is intended. This results in correctly positioning the head which brings the horse back under control quickly. It is also an ideal choice for the horse who throws his head up in the air, as when he does so he will receive an increase of pressure upon his nasal passages which will slightly restrict his breathing. His natural reaction is to lower his head in order to relieve the pressure, which brings it back in to the position of control.

one will permit adjustments to be made on the front nosepiece, as well as the rear strap, although to its detriment this is rarely seen on a drop noseband in current times.

Flash

The flash noseband was designed so that a standing martingale could be attached to a noseband which had a lower chin-strap. It is a combination of both cavesson and drop noseband, but unfortunately it is not as good as either on their own. The cavesson part, even if fitted correctly to begin with, usually ends up sagging under the pressure exerted by the lower chin-strap, which then allows the lower chin-strap to become loose and therefore useless. It has been known on more than one occasion for a horse to go around a showjumping course with the lower strap flapping about in front of his nose.

Fitting
Correct fitting of this noseband is crucial if it is to achieve its aim, and also to prevent the horse from being nearly suffocated. The noseband should sit about 8cm (3in) from the nostrils, but always above the end of the nasal bone itself. The lower strap does up under the bit and sits comfortably in the curb groove. One finger should be permitted between noseband and face all around, giving the impression of a snug fit.

Construction
It consists of a cavesson with a small loop sewn into the front of the nosepiece, through which a longer, thinner strap passes.

Fitting
The cavesson part does up as a cavesson and the lower strap runs diagonally from this,

Use
The drop noseband alters the whole effect of a snaffle bit. Once a contact is taken up with the reins, pressure is exerted directly on to the nose and indirectly on to the poll. This encour-

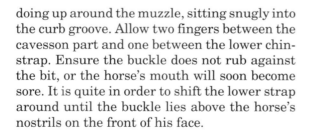

The flash noseband aims to combine the action of both cavesson and drop.

The flash is often used where a standing martingale is also fitted. Note the cavesson part of this flash is covered in sheepskin to offer added protection and to encourage the horse to lower his head on the way to the fence.

doing up around the muzzle, sitting snugly into the curb groove. Allow two fingers between the cavesson part and one between the lower chin-strap. Ensure the buckle does not rub against the bit, or the horse's mouth will soon become sore. It is quite in order to shift the lower strap around until the buckle lies above the horse's nostrils on the front of his face.

Use
The flash does give more control than a cavesson used alone, but less than if a drop is used, as its action is imprecise. The point of pressure is not specific as the whole structure is often unstable due to its shifting in response to movement of the jaws. A broad, strong cavesson part will help to ensure that the lower chin-strap does not entice it downwards, but even so, you may be better off deciding upon the use of either a cavesson or drop on its own, unless it is

critical to have a standing martingale and a lower chin-strap to prevent the horse from opening his jaws.

Grakle

The Grakle is often mistaken for the flash, but is a totally different design. It was named after 'Grakle', the 1931 Grand National winner, who wore one in the race.

Construction
It has two loops of leather which slide through a flat, round, padded nosepiece, in a figure-of-eight design. (Incidentally, it is also known as the *figure eight* or *cross over* noseband.) A good design will have a back strap which lies along the jaw connecting top strap to bottom. In some cases this strap can simply be added, if not already there.

The Grakle is a useful noseband for horses which constantly open their jaws in order to evade the bit.

The Kineton is a good choice for retraining the hard-pulling horse.

Fitting

Although there is a standard fitting the idea of the Grakle is that it can be adjusted to suit individual preferences. The standard fitting is to have the flat nose ring sitting midway between the projecting cheekbone and the bit, on the front of the nose. Each strap is then tightened until it will admit one finger. However, it may be desirable, in some cases, to slide the nose ring upwards, thus shortening the upper strap and lengthening the lower one or vice-versa. This enables the pressure point to be raised or lowered on the nasal bone, which may be desirable to complement the action of certain types of bit.

Use

It is useful on horses who constantly open their jaws and fight the bit, or those who resent the restriction on breathing a drop can

produce. It will allow more movement in the jaw, and can therefore take away that feeling against which the horse is fighting. A gentle pressure is exerted on the muscles around the horse's cheeks which is often enough to discourage him from trying to open his jaws too widely.

Kineton

The Kineton, or 'puckle' as it is often referred to, is becoming more popular, especially on children's ponies. It is a strong noseband and the theory is that if the child can get away with a Kineton without resorting to a more severe bit, then it must be better for the pony. This is sadly not a beneficial attitude as the Kineton is harsh in itself and does therefore need a degree of expertise when using it. If it is pulled on indiscriminately as a braking aid, then the horse will just pull all the harder in order to free himself from the pain he receives as a result. Another drawback is that the child or novice rider quickly learns that a piece of tack can be used to stop their pony, when they should be developing the skills to do so themselves. Relying on harsh tack is never the answer to a problem; nevertheless as long as its action is understood and care is taken with its use, the Kineton is a good choice for retraining a hard-pulling horse.

Construction
It has two rounded metal loops which sit behind the bit-rings, against the horse's face. These are attached to a metal reinforced nosepiece, which should be padded on the surface in contact with the nose. These is no curb-strap and it attaches to the bridle by means of its own slip-head.

Fitting
The nosepiece is adjusted at the front, more to the shape of the horse's nose than for tightness. The slip-head is adjusted until the metal loops are just touching the bit mouthpiece. This should ensure the nosepiece also sits in line with the bit mouthpiece, but in any case it should never sit lower than 2.5cm (1in) above the end of the nasal bone. If it does lie lower than this it could slip off the end and act on the nostrils which would be very painful, severely restricting breathing and serving no purpose at all.

Use
Pressure is exerted on the horse's nose immediately you take up the reins. While he keeps his head down and under control, the contact is light and so the pressure is minimal. However, as soon as he lifts his head, direct, strong pressure is put on to his nose which encourages him to refrain from doing so. It is a good device for use when retraining 'stargazers' (horses who continually go around with their heads horizontal). They soon learn that it is they who control the pressure by keeping their

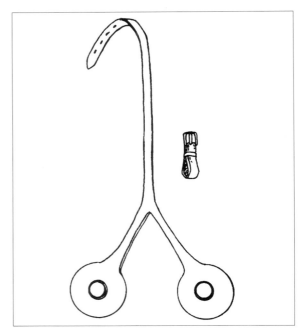

The Australian Cheeker.

head down and thus under the control of your hands, through the bit.

Australian Cheeker

This is most often used on racehorses but could be used on everyday riding horses.

Construction
It is one long length of rubber with circles which slip over the bit-rings, acting like bit guards. The circles which are of leather or rubber slip over the bit rings by lying flat against the horse's face to prevent pinching from the bit. These extend diagonally up the face until they meet at a point on the bridge of the horse's nose, forming into a single strap which runs up the horse's face and attaches to the centre of the headpiece by a small buckle.

Fitting
It is adjusted at the poll until the bit is held high in the mouth.

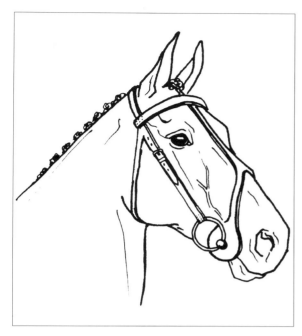

How the Australian Cheeker is fitted.

Use

Its effects are largely psychological because the actual pressure exerted is minimal. It appears to prevent the horse from 'running in to it', acting as a barrier between his nose and the open space in front of him. It does seem to have a good effect on strong pulling horses in this way, and has cured one particular horse from continually bolting, although no one can give a definite reason why this should be so. It does have a practical application, however: that of keeping the bit high in the mouth and so preventing the horse from getting his tongue over the bit.

REINS

Reins are important as they provide the means of communication between you and your horse. While you should not rely on the reins alone in order to guide or stop your horse, without them you would be unable to transmit your intentions (unless you happen to be one of those remarkable riders who can ride without any reins at all). If you think of reins in terms of an extension to your natural aids, your seat, legs, voice, hands and so on, then you are likely to use them sympathetically. Rough use of the reins is a sure way of causing your horse great discomfort, resulting in a breakdown of communication and ultimately resentment.

While all reins serve the same purpose there are things to consider when selecting a suitable pair.

Width

The size of your hands will determine the ideal width of the reins you use. Few people realize that reins can be uncomfortable if they are incorrectly matched to your hands, which has a knock-on effect, leading to a loss of concentration and less effective riding. An average pair of reins is between 1.5cm (⅝in) and 2cm (¾in) in width, but these may be unsuitable if your hands are much smaller or larger than average. If reins are too wide you will be conscious of their bulk between your fingers which may make it hard for you to handle them sensitively. If they are too narrow you will feel as if you do not have a proper hold on them and consequently you will be trying to grip on to them tightly, which your horse will feel as an unyielding contact. Although there are exceptions – for instance, in competition you might want a wide rein to ensure you have a good grip – generally the rule is 'the smaller the hand the narrower the rein', so 'try before you buy'.

Length

The length of reins also needs to be considered, although this is more or less standardized into adult and child categories. Most reins are between 132cm (52in) and 152.5cm (60in), although pony reins are often found between 122cm (48in) and 137cm (54in). The consideration given to length does not affect you as much as your horse. Reins need to be long enough to accommodate the length of your horse's neck and still leave enough room for you to be able to hold them without restriction, or to have a knot tied in them at the buckle end if necessary. This knot is sometimes desirable when riding cross-country as should you need to slip the reins to their full extent in an attempt to provide your horse with enough freedom to stop himself from falling, it will prevent the buckle from bursting apart from the pressure of the reins pulling against his neck. If the reins were not knotted and thus broke in such a situation, your horse could stand on or get tangled in loose trailing reins which could spell disaster. This knot will also enable you to regain control over the reins quickly once contact has been lost.

Conversely, reins which are too long are hazardous to your safety as they may hang down over your stirrup, providing an opportunity for your foot to get caught in the loop. To select an appropriate length of rein for your horse, measure from your horse's withers to its mouth and choose a pair which is 28cm (11in) greater than this measurement. Once riding, this should give you about 23cm (9in) of free rein hanging below your hands, which is ample.

Types and Uses of Reins

Apart from the safety aspects, such as width and length, which need to be considered, you should also give thought to the suitability of the reins for your purpose. Some types of reins are more effective for certain activities, while others are deemed 'correct' for the show ring. Most reins are made of leather, with various designs used to provide a good hand grip, although other materials, from cotton to plastic, are available. Those which incorporate some form of hand grip are left plain at the bit end to accommodate martingale rings and stops, if needed.

Plain Leather
These are not practical for everyday riding as they become slippery when wet with rain or sweat. For this reason it is always sensible to wear gloves when using them. They are usually worn for showing and where two pairs are used on a double bridle, the bridoon rein is always wider than that of the curb to enable you to distinguish easily between the two by feel alone.

Plaited Leather
These start as a plain leather rein at the bit end, which splits into five strands approximately 25cm (10in) from the bit. These strands are then plaited right up to the buckle attachment. Although they do provide more grip than plain leather reins, they too can become slippery when wet, and are also inclined to stretch with use. Plaited nylon reins are a cheaper imitation, but these become lethal when wet and very harsh when dry, so are best avoided.

Dartnall
These are another plaited design, but as they are made of soft, plaited cotton they overcome the problem of slipperiness, unless they are allowed to become clogged with dirt and grease. They are slightly curved to fit the shape of your hands which makes them very light and kind, helping you to maintain a nice sensitive contact with your horse's mouth. Because of their lightness they are ideally suited to dressage and endurance riding. However, you may feel you need something with a little more weight for cross-country riding and showjumping.

Laced Leather
These are often confused with plaited leather reins but are quite different. They are a plain leather rein with a thin leather lace threaded through in a series of Vs to form a hand grip and are therefore more effective than plain leather alone. They are often used as an alternative to the thicker bridoon rein on double

German Web reins are very popular with showjumpers.

bridles in the show ring, as at least they do provide some grip and are unobtrusive.

Rubber-Covered Reins

These are the most popular for general riding and most competitive disciplines as they provide a good grip in all weather conditions. They are basically a plain leather rein with a cloth-backed, pimpled rubber covering which begins about ten inches from the bit and extends along the rein from 50–76cm (20–30in). The rubber hand grips do wear quite quickly, but they are easily replaced by your saddler when necessary for little cost. Ask your saddler to sew by hand down the centre of the rein in fairly wide stitches, as close

machine stitching will reduce the strength of the leather underneath. When buying these reins, or having them re-covered, ensure a long enough length of plain leather is left at the buckle end to tie a knot if desired.

German Web

These are another popular design, because they, too, provide a good grip in all weathers. To achieve this grip, small leather slots are spaced approximately 10 or 13cm (4 or 5in) apart along the the hand areas. They are made of webbing which makes them light and sensitive, so they are an ideal choice when also using a martingale as you can feel the slightest pressure.

3 Bits and Bitting

Selecting the right bit for an individual horse causes many people hours of deliberation and frustration. One horse will go well with only one particular bit for the whole of his life while another may go through a great number until one is found which seems to be satisfactory. Selecting the most appropriate bit is not an easy task: your horse cannot tell you how he feels and so you must make an informed judgement based on his behaviour and way of going. Additionally, the temptation to try one bit after another in the quest for perfection must be resisted, or you will just end up going around in circles. The old saying 'if it isn't broke don't fix it' is most appropriate. While your horse is going well *do not* meddle with his tack. If he does not seem happy, do not automatically assume his bit is the cause; first discount all other possible factors. A horse which seems unhappy in his mouth may have either sharp teeth, sores or even a bad back and, of course, any bit is only as soft as the hands on the other ends of the reins – are your hands soft?

It is often said that there is a 'key' to every horse's mouth, but this 'key' is not a piece of equipment; rather it is correct and sympathetic riding. More complex bits may be needed as the level of schooling or stage of competitive activity increases, but for most purposes a snaffle is quite adequate. The idea is to find the mildest bit which your horse will respect. This will be determined by past bitting experiences and his temperament and ability. Remember that, while it is all very well for idealists to say only strong riders need strong bits, it is foolish to ride your horse out hacking in a mild snaffle if you know that at any given

opportunity he will run off with you. It is far better to use a strong bit mildly, than to use a mild bit strongly. On the other hand, a horse cannot be made to 'go better' by imposing pain on him, so those bits that are designed to do so (and there are still some in use), are better off being used as ornamental curios on some pub's wall, as is currently the fashion.

In selecting a bit for your horse you need to match its action and severity to the desired effect. For example, you do not want to use a bit to raise your horse's head if he goes around with it in the air anyway. Good bitting is all about common sense, and by simply giving your horse's character and action a little thought you can often eliminate the use of certain types of bit without even trying them. However, you should never consider the bit in isolation, as other tack and your own riding skills will greatly influence its action. Correct and constant evaluation of both your horse and yourself is the answer to successful bitting, and a small investment in good tuition may save a huge one in a library of bits.

In general, bits can be divided into three main families: snaffles, curbs and Pelhams, with other related groups, such as gags, having a combined action of two of the families. When selecting a suitable bit for your horse, consider his comfort and your safety. A bit needs to be of the right size, type and weight for your horse's mouth and great care should be taken when fitting to ensure his comfort, but for your safety's sake it also needs to be of the correct strength so that he neither takes advantage of it nor rebels against it. The action of any bit depends upon its design and the horse's head-carriage. The same bit can

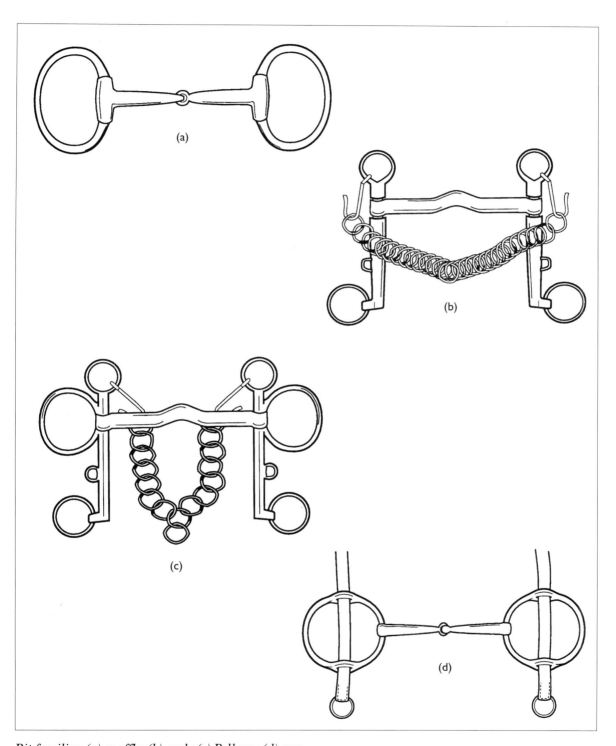

Bit families: (a) snaffle; (b) curb; (c) Pelham; (d) gag.

act on different control points, depending on whether the horse's head is raised or lowered. However, a bit cannot be used to *produce* a desired head-carriage, which is instead the outcome of correct schooling; nevertheless the various types do offer different results when used competently.

SNAFFLE BITS

The term 'snaffle mouthed' tends to conjure up a picture of a well-mannered horse, going in a nice outline with just the slightest pressure felt on the reins. In reality there are over eighty different types of snaffle, ranging from the very mild to the extremely severe, so 'snaffle mouthed' does not necessarily describe a quiet horse.

Factors Determining Action and Severity

The action of different bits varies enormously even to the point where a horse which acts like a 'dobbin' in one bit, and turns into a very nice ride in another. The combination of mouthpiece and bit-rings or cheeks will determine a bit's action; however, it will also be affected by the horse's head-carriage and by the way you hold the reins.

Bit materials play a large part in determining severity, so it is best to decide upon the material first. Stainless steel is the hardest on the mouth, but is the most common and suits most horses. Vulcanized rubber is less severe and is a good choice for the horse with a sensitive mouth, or one who chomps continually at a metal bit. Nathe and soft rubber are particularly suitable for those horses with delicate bars, or those who have unfortunately been the victims of rough treatment though the bit.

Having decided upon the right material, you need to consider the thickness of the mouthpiece. A thick mouthpiece is fairly mild, with severity increasing the thinner it gets.

However, always bear in mind your horse's mouth conformation. If he has a short mouth and a thick tongue he may literally find a thick bit too much of a mouthful, in which case a thinner one would make him happier.

While the type of mouthpiece does determine the action of the bit, various types can be equal with each other when it comes to severity. The difference is in the way pressure is distributed, so success lies in matching pressure distribution to your horse's strengths and weaknesses.

Bit-rings are designed in different ways to provide varying degrees of 'play'. For example, eggbutt rings are fixed to the mouthpiece and offer minimal movement, whereas loose rings allow the horse to move the mouthpiece up and down to a certain degree. Cheekpieces, as opposed to bit-rings, offer a guiding action on the cheeks and therefore are particularly suitable for young horses or for those who have never learned to go 'straight'. One thing is for sure, your horse will soon let you know if he approves of your choice, so 'listen' to him.

Fitting

However mild or severe a bit is designed to be, common sense dictates that it will not be comfortable for the horse unless it fits properly and is adjusted correctly in the mouth. Before you decide what bit may be suitable, look at the size and conformation of his mouth and jaws. Just because your friend's horse goes well in a certain type of bit there is no reason to suspect your horse will also. Bitting is above all individual. Each horse has his own mouth shape: his roof may be high or low, his tongue coarse or narrow, his lips fleshy or thin or his bars sensitive or deadened, so it is not enough to select a bit purely on the desired result. While examining your horse's mouth you may become aware of a problem in conformation and can therefore avoid trouble by not choosing a bit which will act directly on the problem areas. For instance, a horse with a coarse tongue may intensely dislike a bit which operates on tongue pressure, so in this case a double-jointed, or even hanging cheek would be more appropriate than a bit with a mullen mouthpiece.

A common mistake is to have a bit which is too wide for the mouth, which results in the cheeks or rings banging on the sides of the mouth or chafing back and forth in a sawing motion. A jointed snaffle that is too wide will hang lower in the mouth than is desired, possibly banging against the tushes or even incisors and certainly being very uncomfortable. Such a poorly fitting bit will encourage the horse to get his tongue over it and may induce evasions. Similarly, a bit which is fitted too low is another common error and this also encourages the horse to put his tongue over the bit; a habit which once begun is very hard to break.

A bit which is too narrow will also cause discomfort by pinching the corners of the lips. Fulmer cheeked bits can dig into the cheeks of a horse with a broad face, so ensure you choose the type which has the cheeks curved slightly away from the face for such a horse.

As a general rule, a straight bar or mullen mouth bit should sit snugly in to the corners of the lips without wrinkling them. A single- or double-jointed snaffle should sit up into the corners of the lips, wrinkling them slight-

ly. However, as with all areas of tack, common sense should prevail: where a horse's lips are either extra thick or flabby, or his tongue extra bulky, or whatever other way his mouth conformation departs from the 'average', then you must be prepared to make individual adjustments.

To measure your horse's mouth when selecting an appropriate size of bit, hold a piece of string taut in his mouth, with thumb and first finger on each side. Remove the string, measure it and then add on 1cm (⅜in). To check a bit once fitted, make sure you can slip your little finger, but no more, between the bit-cheek and the corner of your horse's lips on each side.

The snaffle group can be divided into different categories depending on mouthpiece and bit-cheek variations.

Snaffle Mouthpieces

Mullen Mouthpieces

These are unjointed and slightly curved. They are the mildest of all mouthpieces, especially if they are made of vulcanite or rubber. A stainless steel one is only mildly stronger, so a mullen bit is a good choice for the sensitive or young horse. Most of the pressure from a mullen mouthpiece is taken on the tongue and the corners of the lips, thus relieving pressure from the bars. This makes it suitable for a horse who resents a jointed mouthpiece, because this does direct most of its pressure on to the bars.

Straight-Bar Mouthpieces

These are unjointed without any curve. They act upon the same control points as the mullen mouthpiece, but their pressure is more direct due to the straightness through the mouth. They can be made of stainless steel, which is the hardest material on the mouth; vulcanized rubber which is less so; and nathe and soft rubber which is very mild.

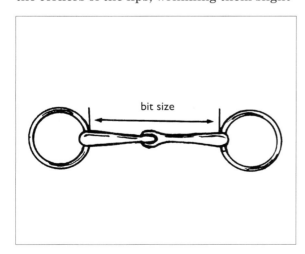

How to determine the size of a bit.

Types of snaffle mouthpiece: top, single-jointed; middle, double-jointed; bottom, straight bar.

Single-Jointed Mouthpieces

These are the sort which produce a 'nutcracker' action. This puts more pressure on the bars, although pressure is also felt to a lesser degree on the corners of the lips, the tongue and mildly on the roof of the mouth depending on the horse's head-carriage. The two arms, which link together at the centre, should be slightly curved, as this allows them to sit comfortably on the bars when the horse's head is in the desired position. The link should allow ease of movement between the two arms, but not so loose that the two arms can rotate.

Double-Jointed Mouthpieces

This type is designed to remove the nutcracker action. Each arm is attached separately to a small centre link, allowing each to move independently. The arms should still be slightly curved and the centre link facilitates each arm sitting on the bars comfortably. Even less pressure is taken on the tongue with this type of mouthpiece, so only the bars and lips are the control points utilized. A good fit is particularly important, so that the centre link lies central on the tongue.

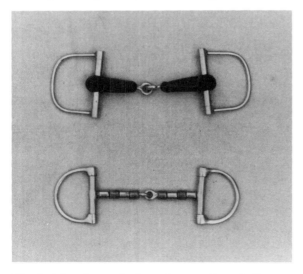

Single-jointed mouthpieces, irrespective of other features, always produce a 'nutcracker' action. Top, D-ring, rubber-covered; bottom, D-ring rollered mouthpiece with alternate copper roller.

Double-jointed mouthpieces aim to remove the nutcracker action. Top, Dr Bristol; bottom, French link.

Ported mouthpieces, like this Fillis snaffle, allow more room for the tongue.

Top: rollered mouthpieces aim to prevent a horse from grabbing hold of them. Bottom: spoon mouthpieces are designed to prevent a horse from getting his tongue over the bit.

Ported Mouthpieces

These have a raised central element to allow more room for the tongue under the bit. This allows the arms of the bit to come directly into contact with the bars of the mouth, so this mouthpiece uses the bars, lips and roof of the mouth as control points. Each arm moves independently of the other so more pressure can be put on one side of the mouth or other, if desired. Where the central element is hinged, each arm can move independently of the other.

Rollered Mouthpieces

These can be either straight-bar or jointed but, as their name suggests, they have rollers over, or incorporated into, the mouthpiece. Their action depends on whether they are jointed or not, although their greatest use is in preventing horses from grabbing hold of, and setting themselves against, the bit. They are also used to encourage the young horse to 'play' with the bit, or to salivate. Copper rollers are sometimes placed alternately with ordinary ones to assist with this.

Spoon Mouthpieces
These have a central plate which prevents the horse from getting his tongue over the bit. There are a wide variety of designs, which may be fixed or movable.

Snaffle Bit-Cheeks

There are a variety of rings and cheeks on snaffle bits. The range includes:

Flat Ring
Not surprisingly, these have flat rings!

Eggbutt Ring
The rings are fixed to the mouthpiece, which consequently makes it immovable.

Loose Ring
The rings slip through the mouthpiece which allows some movement.

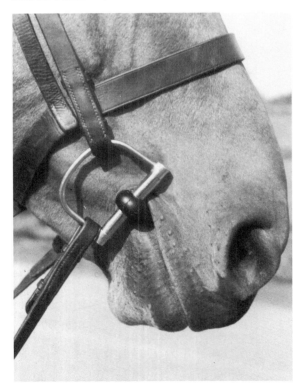

A correctly fitted D-ring snaffle.

D-Ring
These are shaped as 'Ds' to prevent the bit from being pulled through the mouth and to offer a slight guiding action either side of the lips.

Large Ring
The rings are larger than normal to provide security and a guiding action on the cheeks.

Bridoon Ring
This is a small ring, for use on a bit used with a curb to form the double bridle. It may be egg-butt, loose ring or flat ring.

Half-Cheek
The bit has half a shaft running up or down the face.

Full Cheek
The bit has a shaft running both up and down the face from the mouthpiece.

Hanging Cheek
The bit is held up in the mouth from cheeks attaching to the bridle cheekpieces, thus relieving pressure from the tongue and bars.

Spoon Cheek
These are half-cheeks running downwards that end in a bulb, looking rather like a spoon running from the bit-ring.

Types of Snaffle

The snaffle bit mostly acts on the corners of the lips, tongue and bars, although this can vary depending on individual designs and the horse's head-carriage. For instance, where the novice horse works in front of the vertical with a low outline, the action is upward; but where the more experienced horse works with a relaxed jaw and flexed poll, with a higher head-carriage, the pressure exerted by the snaffle is primarily on the lower jaw. Generally, the effect of a snaffle is that of raising the horse's head, although there are exceptions to the rule.

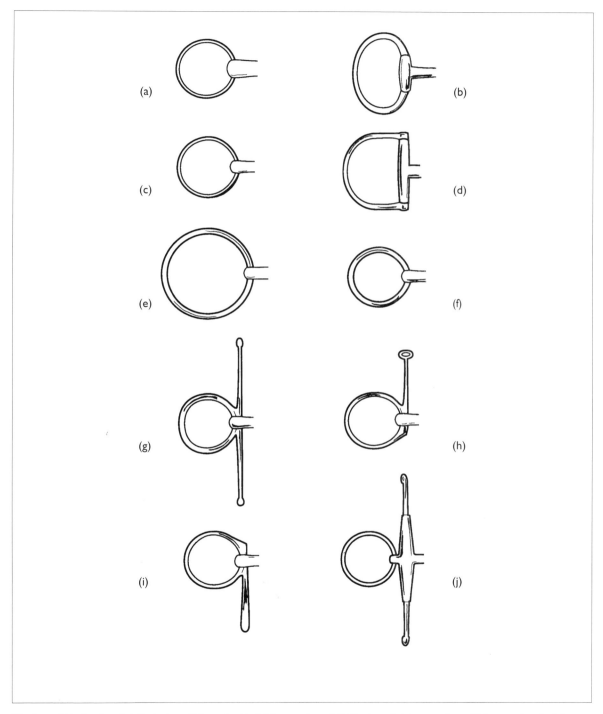

Various bit cheeks: (a) flat ring; (b) eggbutt; (c) loose ring; (d) D-ring; (e) large ring; (f) loose ring bridoon; (g) full cheek; (h) hanging cheek; (i) spoon cheek; (j) Fulmer.

You can ascertain the design and action of most snaffles by choosing the appropriate mouthpiece and bit-cheeks from the above lists. For example, an eggbutt snaffle is a single-jointed mouthpiece with eggbutt rings, so look up single-jointed mouthpieces and eggbutt rings and you have a description and action of the bit. The following is a list of additional information on many popular bits.

Jointed Eggbutt
This is a single-jointed bit with eggbutt rings. It is the most common bit in use and, with a sensible, well-mannered horse, it is adequate for most rider's needs while hacking or schooling. Since the eggbutt rings are fixed they cannot pinch the side of the face or lips. The drawback to this bit is that it can be rather *unfeeling* or *wooden*, and so many riders 'upgrade' to a more sensitive bit when moving into specialist work.

German Snaffle
This describes a single-jointed bit with various cheeks. The bit has a thick hollow mouthpiece and is particularly suitable for horses with sensitive mouths as it has a wide bearing surface and is light in action. It is a popular bit for schooling dressage horses, as requests can be conveyed delicately. It may have eggbutt, or wire loose rings, according to individual preference.

D-Ring
The arms of this single-jointed bit are fairly thin which can make it severe. It is mostly seen on strong-pulling horses and racehorses. The large D-rings prevent pinching of the lips of cheeks.

French Link
This is a double-jointed bit with various cheeks. It has a central peanut-shaped link which lies flat on the tongue, considerably reducing the nutcracker action. It is usually used alone as a snaffle with either eggbutt, loose ring or Fulmer cheeks, but it can also be the 'bridoon' part of a double bridle. It particularly suits those horses who are fussy mouthed as it 'moulds' slightly to the horse's mouth shape.

Dr Bristol
This double-jointed bit, which has various cheeks, has a central plate which lies at about a 45-degree angle to the tongue, unless the horse's head is held on the vertical when it will lie flat. It can be fairly severe as the edge of the central plate will bear on the tongue if the horse is not flexed with a desirable head-carriage. Nevertheless, it does suit many horses who do not respond to curb pressure.

Fulmer
This full-cheeked snaffle, which may be single- or double-jointed, offers a guiding action to young horses. The bit-cheeks are often attached to the bridle cheekpieces by means of little keepers, or 'restrainers'. The top of the cheeks should be angled away from the face to prevent them from digging into the horse's cheeks.

Dick Christian
This is a double-joined bit with loose rings. The central link is a ring which joins the two arms. It is designed to eliminate the nutcracker action and to reduce tongue pressure. It is quite sensitive and therefore is appreciated by a horse with a delicate mouth.

Scorrier
This single-jointed bit has four rings and a blunt, half-denticulate mouthpiece with slots in, through which rings are placed for attachment to the headpiece. The bit also has loose rings for attachment of the reins. When pressure is applied to the reins, the headpiece rings exert considerable pressure on the horse's cheeks and jaw. Its pinching action is severe so this is a bit to be used with caution. It is primarily seen on showjumpers, in a bid to ensure they turn sharply in the ring when required.

The Scorrier snaffle, which can produce a severe pinching action.

The Scorrier is mostly seen on showjumpers in a bid to ensure sharp turns in the jump off (below).

The Magenis snaffle has lateral rollers which afford some sideways play.

Wilson Snaffle
This bit differs from the Scorrier in that its headpiece rings are not fixed to the mouthpiece and are thus able to move along the arms. It can, therefore, have even more of a pinching effect than the Scorrier.

Magenis
This single-jointed bit has loose rings and lateral rollers set inside its jointed arms which are squared off at the edges. These rollers afford some sideways play which can encourage a horse to salivate and prevent him from

crossing his jaws. It is the type of bit horses either love or hate. If it is the right one for your horse you should see a notable difference in acceptance of your contact.

W or Y Mouth

This bit has two, very thin, single-jointed mouthpieces with loose rings, one with a joint set one third to the left of the bit, the other with its joint one third from the right. The idea is that when rein pressure is applied great force is exerted on to a wide area over the tongue. In practice, all this bit does is to pinch the tongue and cause the horse great pain and confusion.

The W or Y mouth snaffle which pinches the horse, causing great pain.

Twisted

The mouthpiece of a twisted snaffle has convoluted ridges running from one side to the other. Severity may differ depending on thinness of the mouthpiece and how smooth or well-defined the ridges are. In any event it is a severe bit which instead of stopping a pulling horse, makes him pull even more to rid himself of the pain. If you feel that because your horse is constantly pulling at you, you need to use such a harsh bit, try (in an enclosed space at first) putting him in the mildest bit you have – it may be that the only thing he is pulling away from is the insensitivity of your hands.

Fillis

This winged, ported bit with half-cheeks is suspended in the mouth, rather than resting on the tongue and bars. Its port allows more room for the tongue. If fitted fairly high in the mouth it can prevent a horse from getting his tongue over the bit.

Belgian

This is a bit which has a cheekpiece made up of three rings, allowing for various rein positions. The mouthpiece may vary. In the top

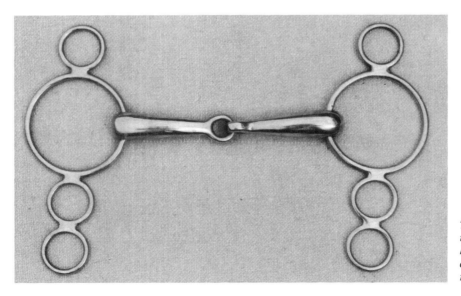

The Belgian 'snaffle', which can have a Pelham or curb action depending on where the reins are positioned.

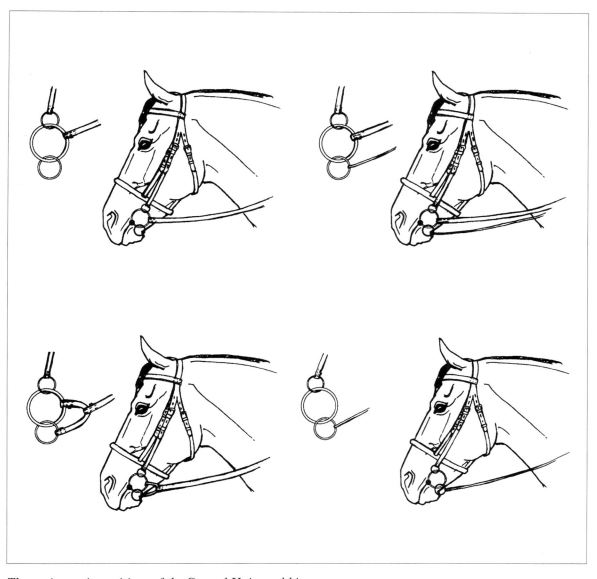

The various rein positions of the Conrad Universal bit.

position the bit is simply a snaffle, but as the rein moves down the rings it exerts a certain amount of leverage on the poll. If two reins are used, it can be used as a snaffle, bringing in poll pressure only if required.

Conrad Universal
Similar to the Belgian bit, this also has a cheekpiece made up of various rings and so can be applied in various ways (*see* above). It can be single- or double-jointed. It is quite a useful bit when jumping as it improves the sensitivity of contact and is helpful when trying to achieve submissiveness. It is also a good bit for more novice riders to use as an intermediate stage when wishing to experience the use of two reins, before advancing to a double bridle.

45

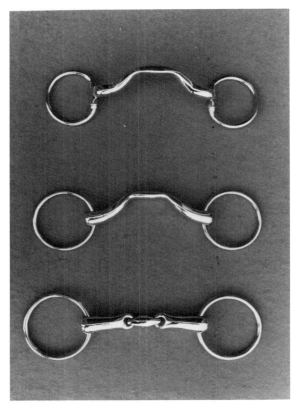

KK bits: top, the schooling bit which is designed to provide a smooth transition between a jointed snaffle and a Weymouth bit; middle, the ported correction bit which allows more pressure to be exerted on the bars; bottom, the mild, double-jointed training bit.

KK Snaffle Bits

KK snaffle bits are unique designs which have been specially adapted to suit the anatomy of the horse's mouth. They are particularly suitable for a horse with a sensitive mouth and can help to prevent, and in some cases overcome tongue vices.

One advantage over many types of bits is that KK bits offer a progressive system. There is a training bit, which has a mild, double-jointed mouthpiece suitable for young horses and those with sensitive mouths. Youngsters about to start their training seem to accept these bits without argument and, if required,

the central link can be made of copper to help the horse salivate. The loose rings also offer a certain degree of play which may be desirable for some young horses. Many horses will not need another bit, but should you find your horse develops a tendency to pull, perhaps when jumping cross-country, the next stage is the correction bit. This has a ported mouthpiece to provide a little extra control, by applying pressure on the bars. It, too, has loose rings and is also helpful when trying to prevent horses from leaning on the bit. The KK schooling bit is popular for more advanced schooling and dressage. It is designed to smooth the transition between a jointed snaffle and a Weymouth and is thus set in a ridged shape which follows the contours of the horse's mouth while the head is held in the correct position. Together with correct riding, an improvement in submissiveness and long-term correction of tongue vices is attainable.

While these bits do provide a progressive system, horses need to adjust to their feel and action, so they should be introduced gradually and only a light contact taken up at first. Once a horse has learned to accept their feel they do seem to settle well, finding the bits kind on the mouth.

Gag Snaffles

Gag snaffles attract a lot of controversy; they are either regarded as a blessing for the otherwise unstoppable horse, or as unnecessary evils, only used by incapable riders. They have certainly become very popular over the last few years which may have something to do with fashion, as many of the top riders now use them in equestrian sports. This is unfortunate, as gags are undoubtedly strong and need competent and sensitive handling. In any case, a gag should not be regarded as an everyday bit, but more as a short, sharp shock where needed.

The gag is technically a snaffle, although it also has a leverage action. Basically, any snaffle mouthpiece can be fitted with gag cheek-

A gag is undoubtedly strong and needs competent handling.

pieces, from the plain eggbutt, jointed snaffle (which becomes a Cheltenham gag) to one fitted with cherry rollers (known as Rodzianko's gag). Instead of the cheekpieces attaching to the bit-rings, they are made of rolled leather and run right through them, terminating in a ring to which the reins are attached. Another rein should also be attached to the bit-ring and used as an ordinary snaffle. When used correctly, the 'gag' action is only brought into play sparingly, as needed. Sadly, all too often you will see people, even top professionals, riding with only one rein and so there is no letup from its effect.

A gag can be very confusing to the horse: firstly the snaffle action asks him to raise his head but when he does so he is confronted with a contradictory downward pressure produced by the gag rein. This does have the effect of making the horse stop and listen, but only when used occasionally. If used continually, the horse will become stiff throughout his back and his head-carriage will be forced. This is especially true if only one rein is used, as then the 'gag' action is always in use and there is no way you can 'give' to relieve the horse.

There are occasions when a gag is the most appropriate bit, but these are rare and certainly not to the extent that we see it in use today. It is a mistake to use a gag on hard-pulling ponies or horses ridden by small children or novice riders, as such riders are unlikely to be able to be able to cope with the two reins or at least manage them with any subtlety. It might prevent the horse from running off if the rider takes a tight enough hold, and produce a quick stopping action as required, but ultimately this will be to the detriment of the horse.

The best use of a gag snaffle is in teaching a horse that he doesn't have to gallop in order to achieve things. It can prevent a horse from running on blindly, and thus make him stop and think about what he is doing. Once he realizes that he can actually jump fences in a controlled way, or canter up a nice grassy slope without boiling over and bolting, the gag should be dispensed with for a more appropriate alternative and only reused as a reminder, if needed.

The gag is also acceptable for the old campaigner who has learned every trick in the book to ignore his rider and do exactly as he wants. Such a horse has probably got such a hard mouth that he will not take notice of any other bit and can be a danger when approaching fences or galloping across country as he will pull his head down in order to get away. The gag will bring his head up and hopefully provide the rider with a safe level of control.

No other bridling accessories should be used in combination with a gag, including martingales and lower strap nosebands. A martingale will prevent the horse from raising his head which is what the bit is initially asking

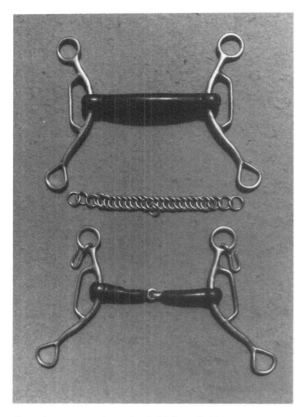

American gags: top, straight bar; bottom, single-jointed.

An American gag has one effect, that of applying poll pressure and thus a lowering of the head.

him to do, while a noseband with lower jaw strap will mean the horse is held in a vice-like grip. Stop and think about what this will do to your horse. Firstly you force him to raise his head, then you sharply pull it down again, only to force it up again; the noseband prevents him from relaxing his jaw which intensifies the effect. If you fit such a combination to your horse, you will be subjecting him to bewildering and harsh treatment.

The American Gag

This is a more severe type of gag, often known as an 'elevator' bit, which has considerable leverage. The term 'elevator' is really quite inappropriate as this bit has one effect, that of applying poll pressure, and thus a *lowering* of

the head. It has a curb rein fitted at the rings at the bottom of the cheeks which can be quite long and so very severe. However, as with all gags, as long as a snaffle rein is also fitted the severe action need only be used if absolutely necessary. It can be useful where a back-up braking system might be necessary, such as when galloping cross-country.

The Hitchcock Gag

This is a complex bitting system which employs two sets of pulleys, one on either side of a specially designed headpiece, and one either side of the bit-rings. The cheekpieces are rolled and most often sewn on to a special loop above the bit-rings. They extend up the sides of the face, pass through the headpiece

The Hitchcock gag.

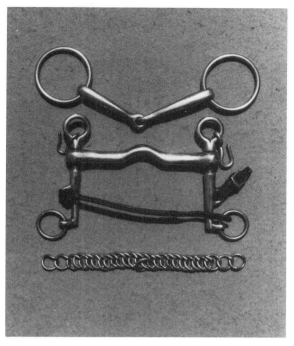

The two bits of a double bridle: top, loose ring bridoon; bottom, sliding cheek Weymouth with lip-strap and double-link curb-chain.

pulleys, run back down the face to the other pulleys on the bit-rings, and then change into reins. It is a very severe system which reacts with lightening speed once pressure is applied to the reins.

Curb Gags

A small ringed gag may be used as the snaffle part of the double bridle in order to raise the horse's head. These are similar in appearance to a normal bridoon, but have the characteristic holes through which the cheekpieces run. The Duncan gag has been specifically designed for use with a curb. The cheek rings have been dispensed with altogether, with the mouthpiece incorporating the holes through which the cheekpieces slide.

The Bridoon

This is the snaffle part of a double bridle. It is, in reality, simply a scaled-down version of an ordinary snaffle and may have various bit-rings and mouthpieces, eggbutt or loose ring, or single-jointed or mullen, for example. Its action is more direct, and the mouthpiece is slimmer, in order to accommodate the curb bit in the mouth as well. Both the bridoon and the curb are controlled independently. The bridoon is fitted slightly higher in the mouth than an ordinary snaffle so that a definite wrinkle can be seen. The curb is fitted some 2.5cm (1in) below this to prevent both bits from crossing over in the jaw, or pinching together.

PELHAM BITS

The Pelham is a much misunderstood and misapplied bit. It is usually seen as an alternative to a double bridle, combining the effects of the bridoon and the curb. However, it is a most valuable bit in its own right,

A Pelham being used in conjunction with a cavesson noseband and correctly fitted, with two pairs of reins.

providing it is used knowledgeably and sensitively. Many horses who do not soften when in a snaffle will be converted when under the effect of a Pelham. Other horses, who have learned to lean on the snaffle, may respond to the action of the Pelham by backing off from it and thus carry themselves properly, rather than relying on you for support. It is often thought to be a strong bit, but this is only when it is used by strong or uneducated hands. The snaffle rein of the Pelham asks the horse to go forward and accept the action of the bit on the bars, while the curb rein, which brings in the action of the curb-chain, asks for flexion. The use of roundings is therefore detrimental to the bit's action and only serves to confuse the horse. It is not too difficult to learn to use two reins well, and the benefit of doing so is that you have to acquire a certain degree of sensitivity, which is, of course, desirable anyway.

The Pelham always applies poll pressure, although this is to varying degrees depending on the amount of contact taken with each of the reins. It also applies pressure on the curb

A divided rein may be easier for the rider to handle as it only means contending with one rein in the hand, but it will produce an imprecise action.

groove, by way of the curb-chain. Other control points, such as the tongue, corners of the lips and bars of the mouth will receive pressure in relation to the design of the mouthpiece, as with snaffles.

There are many Pelham variations, mainly in types of cheek (longer or shorter) and in mouthpieces. Many of the Pelham mouthpieces available are similar to those seen on snaffles (jointed, or mullen, metal or vulcanite for example). The longer the cheeks on a Pelham the more leverage can be applied, and so the more severe the bit. Some people prefer to have more length in the upper cheek section, which then allows more pressure to be applied to the poll, without added leverage.

Types of Pelham

Single-Jointed
This is simply a jointed mouthpiece with Pelham cheeks. The cheeks are usually quite

short and so less severe. It is useful where more control, but not necessarily more severe an action is required.

Mullen Mouth
This is one of the most common types of Pelham used, and is often referred to as the half-moon Pelham. In comes in various mouthpiece designs, the vulcanite mullen mouth being the most common due to its wide bearing surface which suits most horses. It also comes in stainless steel, stainless steel and copper, and nylon and rubber. Some horses will prefer a heavier metal mouthpiece while others will appreciate a lighter one. It is designed to take pressure off the horse's tongue. There is a huge variation in the length of cheeks ranging from the very short, known as the 'Tom Thumb', up to about 19cm (7⅓in).

Rugby Link
This is designed to look as much as possible like a double bridle. Its bridoon ring is linked

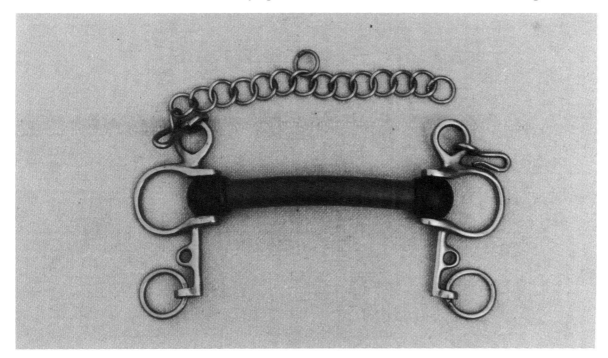

The Mullen Mouth Pelham is one of the most common types in use.

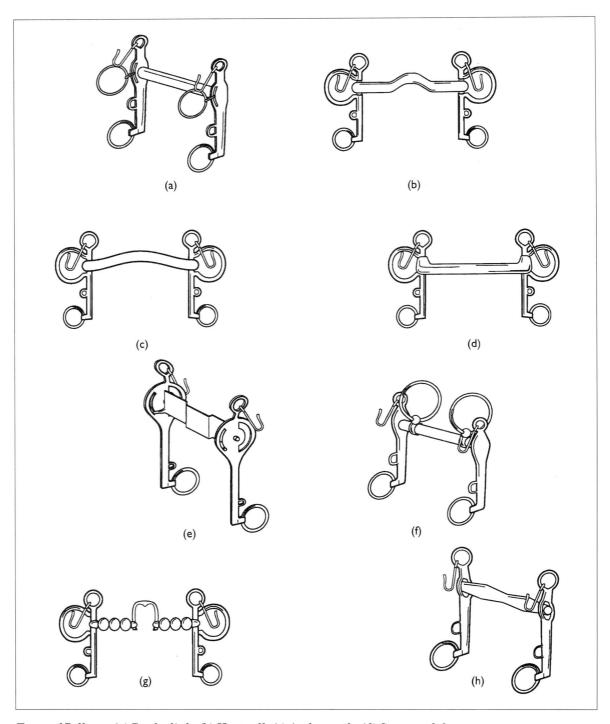

Types of Pelham: (a) Rugby link; (b) Hartwell; (c) Arch mouth; (d) Scamperdale;
(e) SM Pelham; (f) Swales 3-in-1; (g) Hannoverian; (h) Banbury Pelham.

to the Pelham cheek which has the effect of looking as though the horse has both a bridoon and curb in his mouth. It has a definite curb action and is therefore less vague than other pelhams. It is seen most often in the show ring where appearance is all important.

Hartwell

This has a mouthpiece with a tongue groove and is very similar in appearance to the Weymouth curb, although it has an extra ring for the snaffle rein.

Arch Mouth

The mouthpiece of this bit arches upward towards the roof of the mouth to allow the tongue plenty of room and thus pressure is placed on the bars. In contrast, the 'reverse arch mouth' Pelham curves downwards and so places considerable pressure on the tongue. By its very nature it must be severe, and although it may be the only bit to use on a horse with sore bars, such a horse should not be ridden in a bit anyway. Few horses would go well in one and there are far more appropriate alternatives these days.

Scamperdale

This is a straight-bar Pelham which is bent at the cheeks so that it does not rub the horse's mouth or the sides of his cheeks.

SM Pelham

This is a novel design. On appearance it looks very severe as it has a wide flat plate as its mouthpiece which is bent in the middle to form a flat arch. However, as the mouthpiece is on a swivel it never moves from its position; it rests on the tongue and a wide bearing pressure on the bars is, therefore, constantly achieved. The top of the cheeks are angled away from the face so that the swivelling motion does not cause friction on the horse's face.

Swales 3-in-1

This is a strong bit, most often seen on polo ponies. It has wire rings which can slide up and down the mouthpiece, similar in design to the Wilson snaffle. These rings are attached to the bridle cheekpieces and so a very severe squeezing action can be produced. The mouthpiece is fixed and therefore the curb action is very severe, although little poll pressure is applied. It is used in polo to make the ponies turn sharply and stop abruptly, but has little use elsewhere in equestrianism.

Hannoverian

This is a long-cheeked Pelham, which has a ported mouthpiece with cherry rollers set along each arm. It used to be made with a very high port and was therefore unacceptably severe. Nowadays, the port is lower and slightly wider, which allows more room for the tongue and so the bit can act directly upon the bars. It is often used on children's ponies in the show ring.

Kimblewick

The Kimblewick is a modified Pelham in that it does not have a lower shaft and is only designed for use with one rein. It is often seen as a midway stage between a snaffle and a Pelham, for use by riders who do not want to accept defeat and fit a Pelham. However, it is not a question of defeat as the Kimblewick is a very useful design in its own right. It is also known as the Spanish Jumping bit, presumably because it is often used when jumping.

It is suspended in the mouth by way of squared-off eyelets to which the cheekpieces attach. Hooks are attached below these eyelets to which a curb-chain is fitted, and so this bit does offer some leverage and thus a certain degree of poll pressure. The classic mouthpiece for this bit is a straight bar, a ported one (known as a Cambridge mouthpiece) which allows most of the pressure to be taken on the bars. However, there are variations in mullen and jointed mouthpieces, the latter of which, to its detriment, completely changes the bit's action by allowing the curb-chain to slacken and move.

The Kimblewick, a modified Pelham designed for use with one rein.

The 'classic' Kimblewick acts on the poll, curb groove and bars of the mouth and does, in the majority of cases, achieve its aim of lowering the horse's head. Other tack used will also have a considerable effect. A running martingale will intensify its action and any form of noseband with a lower curb strap will interfere with the action of the curb-chain. It can be a strong bit, but not too severe. It is most useful as an occasional, additional brake if needed when hunting or jumping, the horse being ridden in a normal snaffle at other times.

A common variation of this is the Uxeter Kimblewick which has flat D bit-rings with two slots to allow for two rein positions. The theory behind these two alternatives is that with the rein in the higher slots the bit acts as a snaffle with a ported mouthpiece, while the lower slots produce a curb action. In practice, this all depends on the headcarriage of the horse at the time and the same can be achieved by holding the reins higher or lower with the classic Kimblewick. Sometimes, two reins are used together but this serves little purpose.

CURB BITS

The range of curb bits used to be quite extensive, running from the relatively mild to the extremely severe. However, as they have become less fashionable, various designs have faded into obscurity. They usually make up the second part of a double bridle but can also be used in isolation. However, when used alone they can, if not careful, make a horse over-bend as the raising effect of the snaffle is missing. As well as acting upon the bars and the tongue, they exert pressure on the curb groove, poll and to some extent the roof of the mouth, depending on the size of the port. Together with your leg and seat aids, a curb bit will encourage flexion and collection. This is achieved by the combined effect of curb and poll pressure. When the horse feels this effect he drops his chin and flexes in the jaw and at the poll.

Types of Curb

The most common curb bits are the various Weymouth designs and these are the types

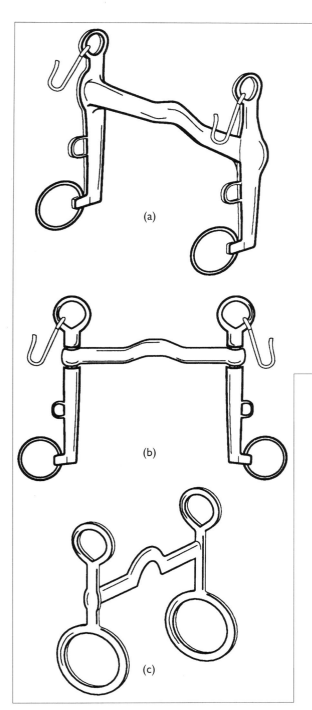

Types of curb: (a) German dressage Weymouth; (b) sliding cheek; (c) globe cheek; (d) Banbury curb; (e) fixed cheek.

most commonly used with a double bridle. Most curb bits have a tongue groove for comfort, although there are other designs. Curb-chains and lip-straps are necessary additions if the bits are to act correctly. Generally the longer the cheek, both above and below the mouthpiece, the more severe the action. Poll pressure can be greatly reduced by having as short a cheek above the mouthpiece as is possible for attaching a rein.

Tom Thumb Weymouth
This has a thick mouthpiece with only short cheekpieces, so is the mildest of all curbs.

German Dressage Weymouth
This has a thick hollow mouthpiece, with fixed cheeks and a Cambridge port. The cheeks are of medium length and, used correctly, it is a fairly kind bit, especially when using it within a double bridle. While it is extensively used for dressage it is also popular for other disciplines.

Sliding Cheek Weymouth

This is the most common type of curb bit that is used with a double bridle. The severity of the action of the bit is governed by the cheek-piece length and the amount of 'slide' there is available, which is usually about 13mm (½in) but can be in excess of this. The slide allows the mouthpiece to ride up in the mouth and thus offers the option of more poll pressure when this occurs. It also encourages saliva-tion and relaxation.

Globe Cheek

As its name suggests, this bit has big 'globe' rings which are at the bottom of a fairly short cheek. This bit is often referred to as a Pel-ham; indeed, it will be called one in many bitting catalogues but as there is no ring for the snaffle rein, a curb it is. Such a snaffle rein would be so close to the curb rein that there would be little point in having one, so only one rein is used. They usually have a fixed, ported mouthpiece, but can also be found with jointed ones.

Banbury Curb

This has a mouthpiece which fits into slots in the cheekpieces, which allow it to revolve and slide up and down. Therefore the cheekpieces and mouthpiece move independently of one another. It has a tapered mouthpiece which allows extra room for the tongue, but never-theless pressure is still greater upon the tongue than the bars.

Curb-chains and Lip-straps

All curb bits should have a curb-chain and lip-strap. Curb-chains come in various designs and materials ranging from single- and dou-ble-link metal ones to leather, elastic, and jodhpur polo (or Cap curbs) which have a cen-tral triangular link.

Single-link curb-chains may be either flat or rounded. It is essential, when fitting them, to twist the links clockwise so that they lie flat against the curb groove. Double-link ones pro-vide a smoother finish and are more comfort-able for the horse, being less likely to pinch him. Both single and double chains have a

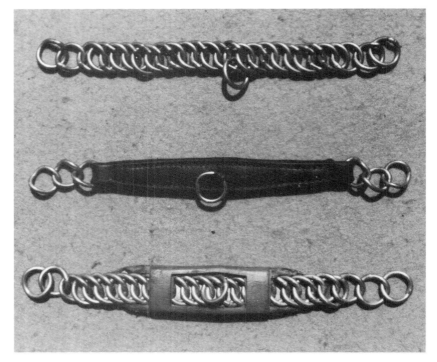

The most commonly used curb-chains: top, double link; middle, leather curb-chain; bottom, double-link with rubber chain guard.

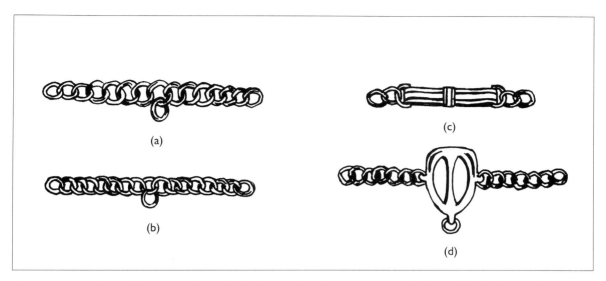

Types of curb-chain: (a) tapered single link; (b) single link; (c) elastic curb-chain; (d) Jodhpur polo.

central 'fly' link through which the lip-strap passes, which is simply a rolled leather strap to keep the curb-chain in place and prevent it from being lost if it should come loose.

Leather curb-chains are soft on the curb groove and are a good choice if your horse seems to resent a metal one. They consist of a band of leather with a few links at either end, and a fly link in the middle. The only part which the horse feels is the leather band.

Elastic curb-chains can be used for a very sensitive horse who objects to the feel of a chain on his curb groove. However, you should realize that this will alter the action of the curb, allowing more 'give' than normal. A better alternative might be a rubber chain guard, which is designed to prevent any form of chafing or friction or, better still, a sheepskin guard which is easily made.

Jodhpur polo curb-chains have a large central rounded triangle which sits midway on the curb groove. It is designed to exert considerable pressure on the lower jaw bone, but often slides up and loses this effect, and when it does so it can dig into the horse's skin.

Fitting

To fit the curb-chain correctly, first attach the chain to the offside hook. Then pass it along the curb groove and twist it clockwise until all of the links are lying flat and the fly link is facing outwards and downwards. You need to judge the tightness of the curb-chain so that it will come into play when the curb cheeks are at approximately a 45-degree angle to the mouth. Take up the appropriate link which will achieve this measurement, and turn it halfway so that the bottom is facing in towards the mouth of the horse. Like this, slip the link over the near side curb hook and this will ensure it stays lying flat against the curb groove.

If the curb-chain is too long, many people slip the extra links over the curb hook as well, or simply leave them hanging. This looks messy and once you have the right measurement for a particular horse, it is far more sensible to remove any excess links. A curb-chain is, after all, a relatively inexpensive piece of equipment, so a new one, for a new horse, will not break the bank.

4 Martingales and Gadgets

The word 'gadget' tends to conjure up all sorts of disparaging thoughts and people often shy away from using them for fear of being classed a failure. However, it is not the derogatory word that purists make it out to be; it simply means a *useful* piece of equipment which make a job easier. Referring to all gadgets as 'training aids' will probably help to lift the stigma, but nevertheless they do need to be used cautiously in the full knowledge of the individual horse's problem or deficiency.

There are two schools of thought when it comes to training aids and two normally sensible people can get into quite a heated argument about it. One person will inevitably feel that they have no place whatsoever in training a horse and will take great pleasure in explaining that all horses should be schooled well enough to jump or behave well without them. The other will be made to feel inferior by this attitude and will be seen doing somersaults in order to explain how they helped with a certain problem their horse had. Because of this constant conflict between the pro- and anti-gadget people, there seems to be increasingly more confusion about just what such aids are and how they work. This results in the average rider being afraid to ask questions for fear of being mocked, so they battle on alone.

If you have a horse that goes well under saddle and in-hand you are unlikely to need the help of any training aids. However, if you have a horse that is behaving undesirably, their use may be beneficial. There are guidelines for the employment of training aids and bearing these in mind at all times will lead to their successful use.

1. Don't rely on training aids as a means of achieving quick results. All you will do is subject your horse to great discomfort.
2. Do try to school your horse correctly first. If this doesn't work, ask the advice of an experienced instructor before using a training aid.
3. Training aids do not 'create' a desired outline, only correct schooling and riding can do this.
4. If you feel your horse will benefit, do use a training aid *but only* if you can use it properly and are experienced enough to be able to gauge when you are getting the right results.
5. Do dispense with the training aid as soon as your horse responds in the correct manner, otherwise he will learn to rely on *it* rather than on *you*.

The key is to bear in mind that all horses are individuals; if you feel it will help a particular horse to understand better what you are asking of him, then training aids will be beneficial.

The use of training aids can be compared to the bringing up of young children. Unless you are able to make children understand what you require them to do, they cannot comply with your requests even if they want to. At best they may make a guess, but it will not be an educated one, and they only have a 50 per cent chance of being right. Horses do not even guess. They do want to please, however, and will get themselves into a panic if they cannot comply because they simply do not understand. If a training aid provides the means of understanding, why not use it? Training aids are often frowned upon for producing quick results but, if used correctly, this is because the horse has understood your requests and complied, not because he has been forced.

There is a danger that inexperienced people will use training aids without really understanding their horse's problem, if indeed he has one; unfortunately, many riders are themselves the problem. Only correct schooling will bring lasting results, which may mean spending money on expert tuition rather than on a piece of equipment. This should not be to the total exclusion of training aids though, which can provide the answers to a host of problems, provided they are used with caution.

MARTINGALES

Martingales are often classed as gadgets even though they are commonly used in many equestrian pursuits and everyday riding. The use of martingales varies but there are three main reasons why they are utilized. Firstly, a martingale is used to prevent a horse from throwing his head in the air. This is a common practice, which stems from the horse being excited or nervous, and very quickly becomes a habit. In such cases, it is only sensible to fit a martingale which will prevent the horse from smashing you in the face.

Secondly, some horses genuinely go better in a martingale. This is because they find comfort in its presence as they know they can rely on it to offer support when needed. They will 'lean' on the martingale seeking to balance themselves on the pressure felt from your hands – it seems to offer them security. Obviously this situation is not ideal, but you must ride your horse as you find him, and if the use of a martingale helps, then so be it; the use of tack is all about being flexible.

The third reason for using a martingale is for a horse who carries his head high on the approach to a jump. Many horses need to do this in order to balance, so using a martingale in order to lower the head may be detrimental. If the horse jumps safely when he arrives at the fence he will probably do better without a

martingale. However, if the horse trips or stumbles because he sees the fence only at the last minute, then a martingale, as a short-term measure, may be beneficial. Ideally, the martingale should be used only to teach the horse to lower his head on the approach to a fence, and then dispensed with once the lesson has been learned. In practice, many horses benefit from constantly wearing a martingale while jumping, for when it is removed they revert to their high head-carriage.

Whatever the reason for using martingales, they must only be fitted to prevent a horse from raising his head above a desired level; not to strap his head down. If your horse constantly tries to throw his head in the air, firstly eliminate all possible causes, such as sharp teeth, an ill-fitting saddle, ear mites or your own riding faults, before employing the use of a martingale.

Construction

There are some features common to all martingales. Each martingale has an adjustable neckstrap which has a slot through which the various individual martingale components run. At the point where these pass through the slot, a rubber ring called a **martingale stop** is fitted diagonally across both straps to prevent the chest strap from hanging down and flapping about between the horse's forelegs. Each chest strap starts as a girth loop. This runs up through the horse's forelegs and through the martingale stop and it is beyond this point that changes occur, making up the various designs.

The Standing Martingale

Fitting
The chest strap of the standing martingale ends in a small loop which is slipped on to the noseband. This loop must only be fitted to a cavesson noseband or the cavesson part of a flash noseband (*see* Chapter 2). If it were

The standing martingale should not interfere with the horse stretching his neck over a fence.

fitted to a dropped noseband it would severely restrict the horse's breathing and would also interfere with the action of the bit. Occasionally, a horse may need the action of both a dropped noseband and a standing martingale. In such cases, and where a flash noseband will not suffice, a cavesson and dropped noseband can be worn together, with the standing martingale obviously attached to the cavesson. Care needs to be taken that the two nosebands do not rub or pinch the skin, and either the standing martingale or dropped noseband should be dispensed with as soon as possible.

To ensure that a standing martingale is fitted correctly, push it up towards your horse's throat and adjust it so that it stops a hand's width away from his gullet. Be prepared to alter this a hole or two either way if your horse has too much freedom or finds it too restrictive. The neckstrap should also be adjusted to allow about a hand's width between it and the horse's neck: too tight and it may interfere with the horse's breathing; too loose and it will allow the horse excess freedom.

Use

This design is most useful for the horse who has learned the habit of violently throwing his head up in the air. If wearing a standing martingale the horse will be prevented from doing this, as once he reaches the full length of the chest strap he will simply be pulling against the girth. Many young horses try various ways of evading their riders, including throwing their heads up. Where a standing martingale is used at the first signs of such evasive attempts, it can persuade them that it is not such a good trick after all, thus preventing it from becoming a rather dangerous habit.

This type of martingale may also prove useful for the horse who throws his head up on the approach to a jump (as opposed to the horse who has a naturally high head-carriage). Providing it is not fitted too tightly, it will not interfere with the horse stretching his neck while in the jumping shape (bascule), and may make the difference between getting over the fence safely or not. If it does appear to affect the way the horse jumps, it is probably too tight and you should let it out a hole or two.

The Running Martingale

Fitting

The chest strap of the running martingale splits into two forks just after the martingale stop. At the end of each fork there is a metal ring through which the reins pass. A **rein stop** made of leather or rubber must be placed about 15cm (6in) away from the bit on each rein to prevent these rings from becoming caught on the rein fastenings or bit cheeks.

To check the fit of a running martingale once in place, pull the rings towards the pommel of the saddle and adjust the chest strap until the rings stop about 10cm (4in) away from the withers. Make sure you do this with the girth loop secured, otherwise the chest strap will pull around your horse's neck. Once you take hold of the reins when riding, the martingale rings should not affect the straight line of the rein from your hand to the bit. If the rings exert a slight downward pull, it is fitted too tightly. Correct fitting is all important: too loose and it will have no effect; too tight and it will have a constant pull on the bit through the reins which your horse may strongly object to, and will interfere with the degree of pressure you wish to apply.

Use

The running martingale is the most popular design in use today as it is less restrictive than the standing martingale. It is quite safe as long as it is fitted well, as its action only becomes apparent when your horse lifts his head above the desired angle of control. You also have more control over its action. If for any reason you want to allow your horse more freedom with his head you need only slacken the reins. This is particularly beneficial when jumping and is why you will see most showjumpers and event horses wearing them. On the approach to the fence you can hold your horse up, and then allow him to stretch

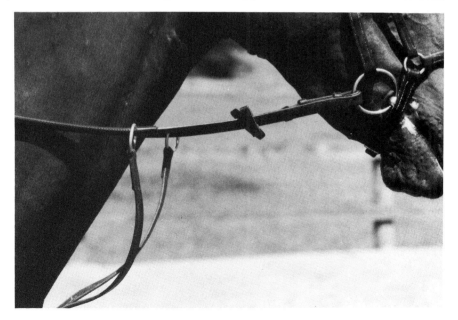

When using a running martingale it is necessary to place rein stops on the reins between the martingale rings and bit cheeks.

The running martingale is useful for jumping as you can hold the horse up on the approach to the fence, but allow him as much stretch over the fence as he needs.

over the jump, regaining complete control the moment he lands.

Go into many riding schools and you will also see various horses wearing running martingales. This is not because they are disobedient in any way but because they have sensitive mouths. The running martingale does help to keep the bit steady in the mouth, which to some extent helps to desensitize the snatches and loss of contact on the rein which are inevitable traits of the beginner rider.

It is possible to use a running martingale to produce an action similar to that of draw reins. Two reins are attached to a snaffle bit, with the running martingale acting on the bottom rein. It is fitted about two holes tighter than normal, so that it does have a downward pull on this rein. You hold the reins as if you were riding in a double bridle so that you only bring the lower rein, and thus the running martingale, into action when you take up a

contact with it. When you do so, the martingale makes contact with the bit, which then acts in a downwards direction on the bars of your horse's mouth. While your horse has his head in the desired position you need not use the lower rein, but it will always be there should you require it. Occasional use of a running martingale in this fashion is beneficial if your horse has become used to relying on it for support when used normally.

A running martingale can also be used with a Pelham or double bridle. If it is being used as a precaution against the horse throwing his head up sharply, it should be fitted to the snaffle rein. If being used as a remedial device when schooling a horse to encourage him to lower his head and work in a lower outline, it should be fitted to the curb rein as it will enhance its action. The action of a running martingale is further intensified when used with a jointed bit, rather than a straight-bar or mullen mouthpiece.

TACK TIP

Check the metal rings to ensure that they are free from flaws at the join. If buying second-hand, discard one that has rust on its rings as this will prevent free movement along the rein and may also mean the rings are not as strong as possible.

The Bib Martingale

The only difference between a running martingale and a bib martingale is that the latter has its two branches joined by means of a triangle of leather, closing in the open space between. This design is used on horses who have learned they can grab hold of one or other of the branches between their teeth, resulting in broken tack, a panicking horse or, at best, loss of the martingale's effect.

The Combined Martingale

As its name implies, this is a combination of the running and standing martingale. It has

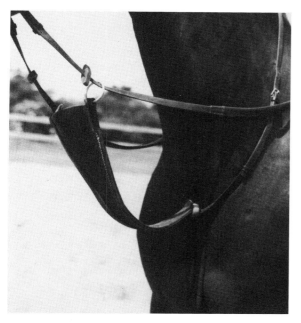

The bib martingale has its two branches joined by a leather section.

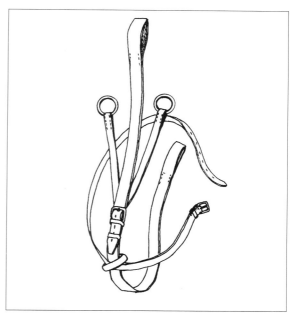

Combination martingale.

The combined martingale has the action of both standing and running martingale, neither of which should interfere with a horse while stretching over a fence.

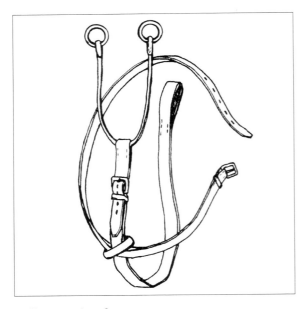

Pulley martingale.

both the noseband loop and rein attachments and therefore incorporates the action of both. It is helpful if both chest-strap attachments are fixed separately, as then one or other can be removed as necessary to leave either a normal standing or running martingale.

The Pulley Martingale

The pulley martingale is another modification on the running martingale and is an extremely sensible design. The chest strap ends in a small loop through which a cord with a ring on each end passes. The reins then run through these rings. This design has the advantage over a standard running martingale in that it allows lateral movement. The horse can bend his neck sideways without causing a pull on the opposite rein. This is most useful when in a jump-off in the showjumping ring, or where tight turns are necessary such as on the gymkhana field.

Take care to ensure the cord is thin enough to slip back and forth through the loop without hindrance. However, it obviously needs to be strong enough not to snap under pressure.

The Market Harborough

Fitting
The Market Harborough bridges the gap between a running martingale and draw reins, and is an extremely useful device. As with the running martingale, the chest strap splits into two branches just past the martingale stop. These branches are twice as long as the running martingale straps, ending in snap hooks. These snap hooks pass through the bit-rings on either side of the horse's head and attach to a rein with a number of D-rings spaced along it, which is designed for the purpose. Lengthening or shortening the branches is easily accomplished by selecting the appropriate D-ring to clip the snap hooks on to, which must be equal either side. In common with all martingales, fitting is extremely important. If, while the horse stands with his head relaxed, the snap hooks are pulling on the bit then they need lengthening. Once fitted, lift your horse's head to a point just in front of the vertical where the rein should have no slack in it and just start to pull on the bit. While your horse has his head in an acceptable position the rein should be slack.

The advantage of the Market Harborough over other martingales is that the horse operates it himself. If he lifts his head, a downward pressure is exerted on the bit, but as soon as he lowers his head this pressure is withdrawn. Horses discover this quickly and soon stop lifting their heads above the angle of control.

How the Market Harborough is fitted.

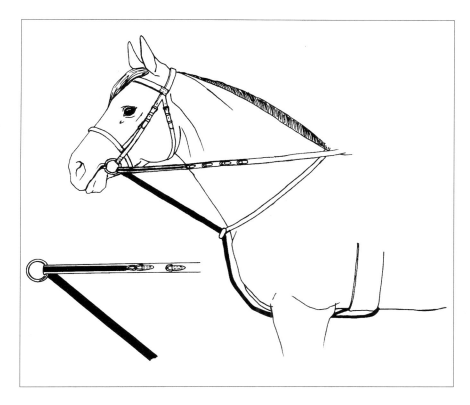

Irish Martingale

The name Irish martingale is a little confusing as this is not a martingale at all. It is simply a short, stout piece of leather with a ring on either end. These slip on to each rein and hold them together. They are mostly used on racehorses, where in the event of a fall the reins stay on the horse's neck rather than being flung over his head and left trailing along the ground.

Less Common Designs

Various designs have appeared over the years in response to one evasion or another. They are not suitable for everyday use and may be hard to find as they are no longer commonly employed. While they have been known to help a horse understand what is required of him, they are often a last resort – a 'kill or cure' approach – and their action can be very severe.

They are best used under professional supervision, and only then if a suitable alternative cannot be found.

The **Grainger** martingale is a cross between a dropped noseband and a running martingale. The two martingale branches extend up to the noseband and attach to its rings on either side. As a result, there is a constant pressure on the horse's nose. The noseband is positioned midway between that of the cavesson and dropped noseband. This type of martingale is often used as a last resort on strong horses, but contrary to all that is sensible with common designs, it does indeed strap the horse's head down. It has little, if any, value, other than when a professional trainer decides to take drastic measures with a particularly difficult horse.

Some martingales such as the **Cheshire** and **Whalley's pattern** attach directly to the bit. For obvious reasons these are unacceptable in modern-day horsemanship.

TRAINING AIDS

It is at this point that 'gadgets' become controversial because the following are used as schooling aids and corrective devices. The aim of such items is to transmit to the horse the way in which you want him to work, thus developing his back and neck muscles, which in turn improves his balance and overall carriage and movement. Some people class training aids as acceptable, but only in expert hands, while others agree that if used competently under supervision they can be of help to the average rider. They are probably of most benefit to the rider of above average riding ability who has to work alone for most of the time. The truth is that there is no definitive answer as to what is helpful and what is not, as each horse is an individual so each problem needs individual solutions. One sure thing is that doing things 'by the book' is only helpful if your horse has read the book first!

Most people use training aids to break through a barrier, when they reach a deadlock situation with their horse and extra help is needed. In such a situation the use of aids can break through the wall of confusion. They can convince – not force – a horse that it is easier and more comfortable to work in a certain way, as if you are translating something which initially he did not quite understand.

As long as you take the time to use them properly and fit them correctly, training aids can be a beneficial way of releasing the answers that the horse already has inside him but just does not know how to access. However, a word of caution: do not attempt to use them unless you have learned what a 'correct outline' is or you may exacerbate the problem and even cause great damage to your horse.

All training aids must be introduced gradually, and only those designed for ridden work should be used when riding and those for in-hand work when lungeing, unless (as a few are) they are designed for both activities. They should only be used with snaffle bits, not curbs or Pelhams as this would make them too severe in action.

All training aids are for short-term use only. Once the desired goal has been reached it is essential that you cease using the aid and work your horse correctly through your own riding ability.

Side Reins

Side reins are the most common lungeing accessory and have become accepted as standard equipment on youngsters when introducing rein contact. They run from the girth straps under the saddle flap or from a training roller to the rings of the lungeing cavesson, initially, and then to the bit. When introducing them have them really loose so that all the horse has to become accustomed to is their weight. Then gradually shorten them one hole at a time until the horse begins to seek a contact with them. *Never* shorten them in order to place the horse's head in the 'correct' position and always ensure they are equal on both sides. If side reins are not used sympathetically they will produce a horse which is stiff and overbent as they will not allow him to stretch forwards when attempting to lower his head.

There are various designs, from plain leather ones to those with elastic or rubber ring inserts. The latter types are intended to provide the horse with a little bit of give, rewarding him if he seeks contact with them. Some horses learn to snatch at these however, so use plain leather ones at the first sign of this happening.

Running Reins

These also attach to the sides of the girth, just below the saddle panel, and are usually made of web. They then run through the bit (from the inside to the outside) directly into your hands. A direct rein is also needed. The effect of running reins is to tip the horse's nose inwards; they have little, if any, effect

Running reins.

on lowering the head via the poll. A variation of the running rein was devised to overcome this issue. It runs from your hand, through the bit, up over the poll down through the opposite bit-ring and then back to your other hand. As soon as you take any contact with this variation, pressure is exerted on the poll and the bit is lifted in the mouth, encouraging the horse to relax his jaw, lower his head and flex at the poll.

Draw Reins

Draw reins run from the girth, through the forelegs, through the bit-rings to your hands. Their action is that of suggesting to the horse that he lowers his head, but they must not be so tight that he is forced to do so. They are always used with an ordinary rein, known as the 'direct rein' so that you take up a contact with them only if and when necessary, relaxing them when your horse responds by relax-ing his jaw and lowering his head. However, you must ride from the leg into the hand, oth-erwise your horse will simply tuck his nose in and leave his quarters dragging along behind.

Draw reins are mostly used when riding, but they can also be of benefit when lungeing *if used with caution*. They run from the girth, up between the horse's forelegs and are secured around run-up stirrup irons on the saddle. When working a horse on the lunge in this way he will pull against himself if he opposes working in a rounded outline, but will reward himself if he works correctly.

Incorrect use of draw reins can be disas-trous, producing tension and pain. Recent studies have indicated that poor use of draw reins may cause a variety of undesirable con-ditions, from headaches to lameness and even breathing difficulties. If you think your horse will benefit from draw reins but are unsure how to fit or apply them, get help from some-one who understands their use.

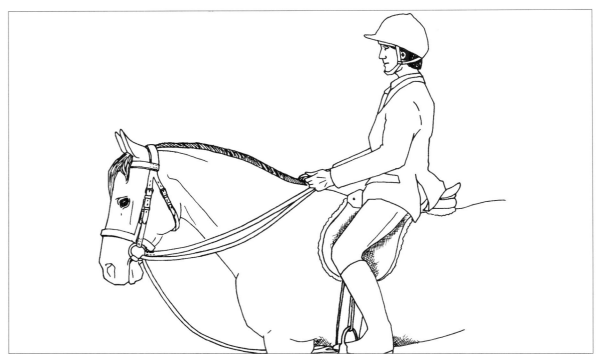

Draw reins.

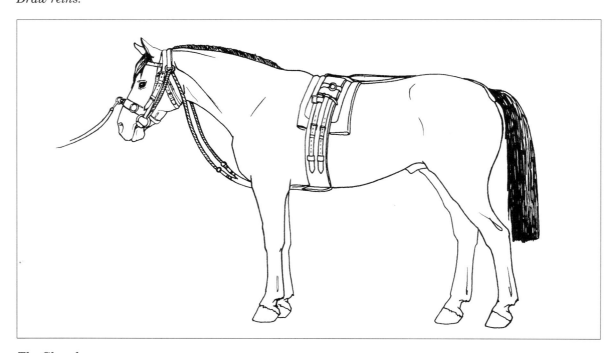

The Chambon.

The Chambon

The Chambon is used only when loose-schooling or lungeing. It comprises a strap which runs from the girth and splits into two with a snap hook on each end. Initially, these snap hooks fix to a specially designed headpiece with a ring at each end and then, when the horse is ready, extend down on to the bit.

The Chambon is especially useful where a horse learns to come behind the bit when lunged in side reins. It is also very effective in correcting horses which, because of going in a hollow outline, have undesirably built up muscles on the underside of the neck. If the horse comes behind the bit, pressure is exerted on the poll encouraging him to stretch his head downwards. If the horse raises his head, pressure is again exerted on the poll and his mouth, thus still encouraging him to stretch his whole top line. As soon as he does so the pressure eases. In this way, a horse soon learns to work in a long but rounded outline

The Chambon is effective in correcting undesirable muscle development on the underside of the neck.

and to adopt a regular and rhythmic gait which is always desirable when lungeing and training horses. Once the horse understands what is required, you can leave off the Chambon and work towards this outline without it.

The de Gogue

The de Gogue offers a system of training which aims to bridge the gap between the Chambon and ridden work. In can be used when loose schooling or lungeing in what is known as the 'independent' position, or when undertaking ridden schooling in the 'command' position.

In the independent position the de Gogue is secured at the girth by a loop. A single strap then runs up between the horse's forelegs and ends in a breast ring. Through this ring a pulley strap is placed with one ring on one end and two on the other. Two reins are fixed by means of snap hooks to the single ring. These reins then run through a ring each on either side of the headpiece, down though the bit and then clip on to each of the two rings on the other end of the leather pulley strap, thus forming a triangle between chest, poll and bit (*see* illustration overleaf).

As with most training aids, as long as it is correctly fitted the effect is of self-operation. If the horse lifts his head, pressure is felt on the bit and poll, thus encouraging him to lower it once again. Once he does so the pressure is released.

Fitting
Having put on the de Gogue, shorten the rope cords (usually done at the chest strap between the horse's forelegs) until they take up a contact with the bit while the horse has his head relaxed. Once your horse is working through you may find this fitting too loose as he will be rounding his back and neck, therefore, you may need to shorten it slightly so that his head does not come up too high. A stop is placed on the rope cord just in front of the headpiece ring, thus removing the possibility

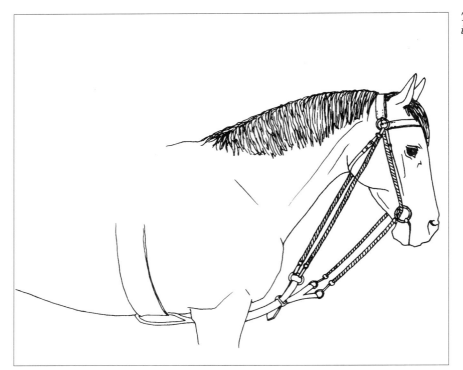

*The de Gogue –
independent position.*

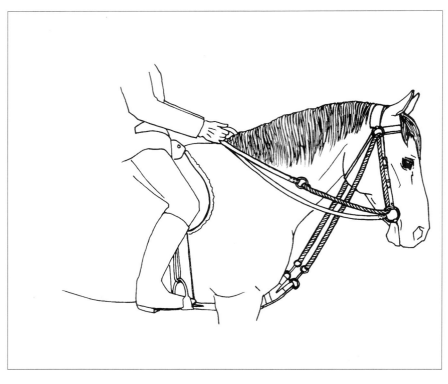

*The de Gogue –
command position.*

of the horse over-bending. Always be governed by your horse's reaction: if he is fighting it, consider whether it is too tight; if to the trained eye it seems to be having little effect, make sure that it is not too loose.

In the command position, instead of the rope cords running back down to the chest pulley strap, they go directly into your hands. Extension reins are needed for this purpose and the snap hooks simply clip on to these. A pair of direct reins are also needed so that the de Gogue's action is applied only when deemed appropriate. In this position, the aid is not operated by the horse but by the rider. It is perfectly in order to jump in a de Gogue, providing you are skilled enough to 'give' with the hand over a fence.

As the de Gogue progresses in a logical way from in-hand to ridden work it is often used throughout a young horse's training. From the start, he has become accustomed to its action and therefore knows the required response.

This can directly result in preventing many of the resistances that are commonly seen in poorly trained young horses.

Abbot-Davies Balancing Rein

The 'Abbot-Davies', as it is commonly known, is an ingenious design incorporating a pulley system (*see* illustration). It was developed in the 1970s by the late Major Peter Abbot-Davies whose theory was that a horse was unable to work in a proper outline unless his muscular structure was sufficiently developed. Thus the balancing rein was devised to achieve this aim.

Spring-loaded pulleys are attached to the bit and through these the reins pass, running from a fixing point on the direct rein to the girth, or tail, depending on the position being used. The reins used are specially designed for the purpose. The balancing rein can be used in three positions:

The Abbot-Davies balancing rein in the initial position.

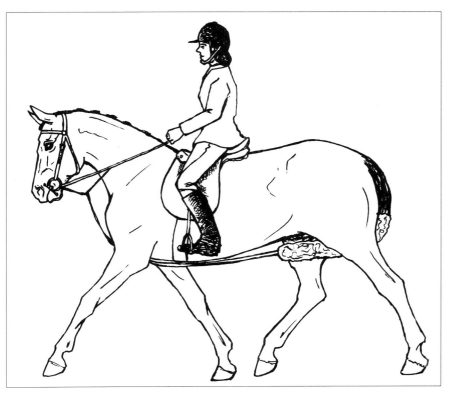

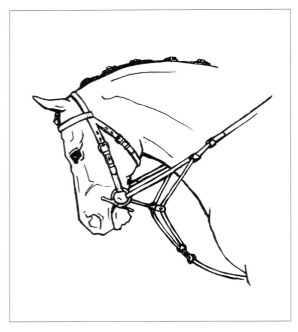

The Abbot-Davies in the 'everyday' position.

progressive stages, and is projected to achieve good results over a period of about three months.

When the rein was first introduced, many people were shocked by it as in its first stage the horse's head is fastened to his tail, thus employing the technique of 'tail reining'. This is where the tail is manoeuvred to encourage the horse to engage his quarters. It has the advantage over normal draw reins in that they only operate on the front end of the horse, where the Abbot-Davies works on the horse from both ends. The desired result is that of a horse with a lowered neck, flexed poll, raised shoulder and an overall rounded top line. In the main, it does seem to achieve these results, and because the horse's muscles have been correctly developed his overall balance is also improved.

1. From the direct rein, through the bit pulley to the tail, which is used to introduce the horse to the aid.
2. From bit to poll, usually used when lungeing.
3. From the direct rein, through the bit pulley to the girth, the 'every-day' use.

It is another aid that can be used in-hand or when riding and working on a system of

---
TACK TIP

Accounting for the fact that not everyone understands the construction or use of training aids it is not unknown to find them poorly made. Many companies have produced such aids and market them under their original names, but unfortunately they do seem to have strayed from the original patterns. When buying one, you must therefore be cautious and insist on your money back if it does not fit or is not properly constructed. A poorly made training aid is certainly worse than no training aid at all. All training aids should come with direct instructions on fitting and use; if they are missing ask for them.

---

5 Saddles

There is far more to selecting the right saddle than you might think. Firstly, you have to choose one which is the appropriate type for your chosen activity, whether it be showjumping, endurance riding or simply hacking. Then you have to ensure that it fits your horse and yourself perfectly. An ill-fitting saddle can seriously affect your horse, causing problems which range from irritability to muscle damage and which soon lead to poor performance. Furthermore, the wrong saddle can have a negative effect on your position and on the way you ride, and may cause backache or more serious problems if you ride a great deal in it.

It takes time to find a saddle that fits both you and your horse, so don't expect to walk into a saddler's and find the perfect one straight away. Generally you will know what you are looking for, either a general purpose, jumping or dressage saddle, for example. Then you will look towards the style: one with a deep, or flat seat, one which has both thigh and knee rolls, one that is dark tan or black, and so on. The choice is endless, but the main consideration is quality. It cannot be stressed enough that quality is everything when buying tack, whether new or used. New saddles will bear a national standards mark, which in the UK is the BS6635. Look beneath the surface. Stirrup bars should be made of stainless steel and quality saddles will bear a maker's nameplate. It is always worth buying from a reputable saddler who will want to come and fit the saddle to your horse himself. Let him; saddles are an expensive investment so you want to prevent costly mistakes. In all cases, beware the saddle that is presented to you cheaply without any offer to fit it to your horse.

Quality used saddles are always better than inferior new ones, but beware if buying at sales and auctions.

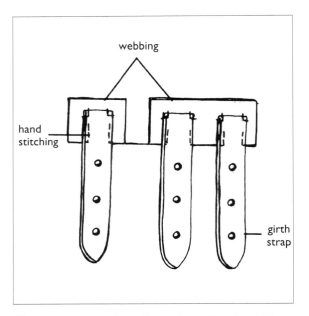

The girth straps of a well-made saddle should be attached to two separate pieces of webbing.

USED SADDLES

A quality used saddle that has been maintained correctly is a better investment than an inferior new one. When assessing a used saddle look for the possible dangers:

• Rust on stirrup bars. This indicates that the bars are probably not stainless steel and may snap under pressure. The adjustable head should also be down, not rusted into the up position.

• Weak or very worn webbing at the top of the girth straps. The girth straps should be attached to two separate pieces of webbing, making a fail-safe system if one gives.

• A broken or damaged tree. Try pushing the two sides of the front arch together; if they move (apart from slight flexion in a sprung tree), it is probably broken. If the cantle can be rocked back and forth, then, again, there is probably a break somewhere.

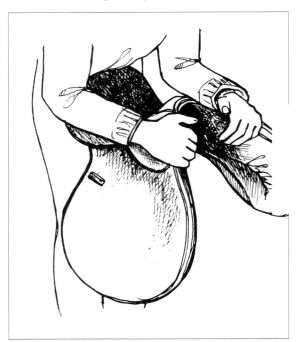

Testing for a broken tree.

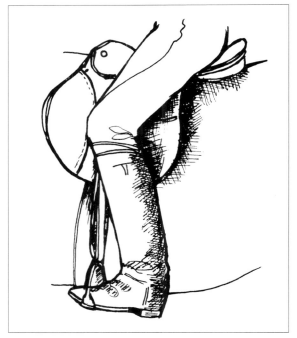

The general purpose saddle will be comfortable enough for riding-club activities.

• Panels that are inadequately or badly stuffed. They should be stuffed with proper flocking (natural or synthetic wool fibre) so that they can be altered to cater for changes in your horse's body condition.

• Lack of balance. The saddle should be clearly symmetrical: when viewing from the back both panels should be of exactly the same depth and shape.

WHAT SADDLE FOR WHAT PURPOSE?

Information concerning the advantages and disadvantages of each saddle type and the many different variations within a type could fill this whole book, but the important point is what do you actually want the saddle for? If you do a little bit of dressage but mainly ride for pleasure, it would be unwise to buy a cus-

tom-built dressage saddle. However, if you showjump many times a week, a purpose-built showjumping saddle will obviously be a good investment for improved performance. How and where you sit on your horse matters a great deal because it will affect the way your horse moves, so a saddle which puts you in an upright position for cross country, or in a forward position for dressage, will detract from the effectiveness of both horse and rider.

Down the centuries, the basic saddle shape has changed little although, throughout the range of saddles available, refinements to help riders in all of the disciplines have been developed.

General Purpose

The general purpose ('GP') saddle is a 'jack of all trades' which will be comfortable and effective enough for the average rider to do most

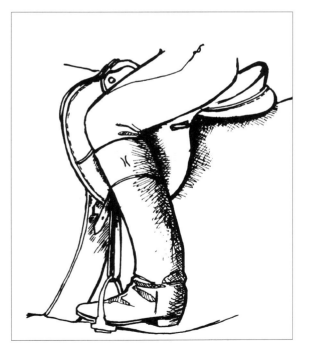

Showjumping saddles accommodate the shorter stirrup length and more forward knee.

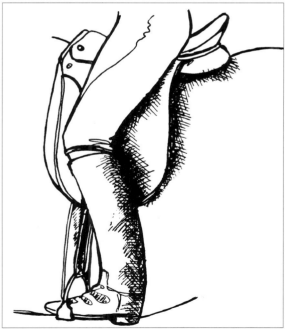

The panel and flap of a dressage saddle is longer than normal to allow for the longer stirrup length required when performing complicated dressage movements.

A typical show saddle with fairly straight-cut flaps and flat seat.

A jumping saddle will be an excellent investment if you intend to jump over larger tracks.

riding-club activities. It is a compromise between a jumping saddle and a dressage saddle, although most have a slant towards one or the other.

There is a huge choice available in terms of style, size and colour, so all the varying priorities of different riders can be catered for. Selecting an appropriate one may take some time, but, to safeguard yourself, strongly consider buying a 'brand name' saddle. If you do buy such a saddle and something should go wrong then, if nothing else, to protect their reputation the makers will put it right. Whether buying new or second-hand go to a reputable saddler, who in the UK will be a member of the Society of Master Saddlers or at least of the British Equestrian Trade Association, both of which have a code of conduct to which their members must adhere.

Most GP saddles are fine for jumping courses of up to BSJA Newcomers height (107cm/ 3ft 6in), but if you go beyond that level you should seriously consider investing in a specialist jumping saddle.

Jumping

A good jumping saddle will offer security and peace of mind, which can boost your confidence when coming down to a big fence. When using a jumping saddle over larger fences you will notice that you will not get thrown forwards as much, especially if your horse has very little in front of him but a powerful rear end!

Showjumping saddles have a rounded, more forward cut panel and flap to accommodate the shorter stirrup length which results in a more forward knee. Additionally, the knee rolls are more pronounced so that the knee can fit snugly when in this position. There is no 'optimum' depth for a showjumping saddle; the seat is chosen purely to satisfy personal preferences; some riders like deep seats, others prefer more shallow ones. Similarly, the length of the seat needs to satisfy the rider.

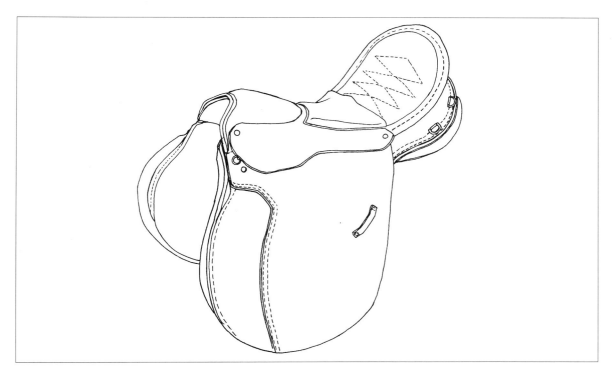

A good type of endurance saddle.

Dressage

On the surface, the dressage-saddle market appears to be a maze of seats, panels and girth-strap designs. The manufacturers know that once a rider has reached a level where a specialist saddle is required they will want one which is going to suit them personally. Rider A wants a deep seat with a long panel; rider B wants a more superficial seat with a longer panel; rider C wants a deep seat with a medium panel… and rider Z wants a combination of four types of saddle in one! The result is a flooded market and a very confused first-time buyer. However, it is important to persevere with the quest of finding the one that suits you best, so do not give up and compromise by choosing one that is only nearly right. A good aphorism for the dressage saddle is 'if it feels wrong then it isn't right'. The right saddle will heighten your performance in the arena, while the wrong one will certainly

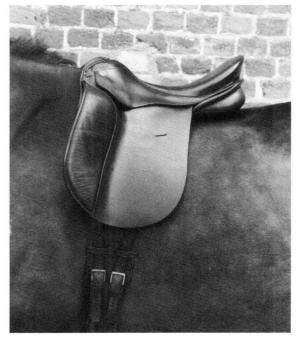

A good dressage saddle will assist your position in the saddle, allowing you to sit long and deep.

diminish it. If you have real dressage ambitions and a horse that is capable of achieving them, it will pay you to go to a specialist saddler and have a saddle custom-made if you can afford it.

In order to allow for the longer stirrup length needed when performing complicated dressage movements, the panel and flap of a dressage saddle are longer than those of the all-purpose design in order to help you towards a more classic riding position. The stirrup bars also place the leathers further under your seat, which helps you to achieve a more upright position. Many saddles also have adjustable bars which allow you to vary the leather position from standard, to intermediate and advanced as you progress. Fur-

thermore, the knee and thigh rolls are so placed as to assist your position in the saddle, keeping your leg supported and allowing you to sit long and deep. Many dressage saddles have two long girth straps for use with a Lonsdale 'belly' girth. Such a girth helps to remove bulk from under the saddle which is desirable for close-contact riding.

If you are an event rider looking for a dressage saddle, your needs may be completely different from the pure dressage rider. You will not be sitting in it for very long so will not have adapted your position to accommodate the very straight flap of some pure dressage saddles and your position demands on the saddle will be less. A saddle with a less straight-cut panel may be more suitable for your needs.

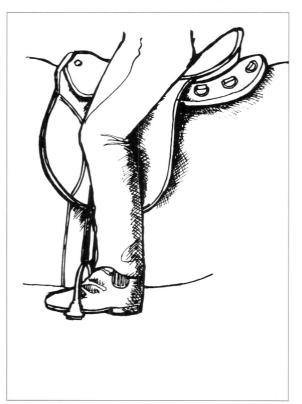

A good endurance saddle will allow for a long leg which helps in achieving an independent seat as the horse goes forward on a free rein.

Event saddles are a compromise. They will allow you to compete in all phases adequately without investing in two different saddles, but will not give the optimum performance of individual styles.

Eventing

Traditionally, the cross-country phase of eventing was ridden in an all-purpose saddle, with a slant towards the jumping style. However, as eventing has become highly competitive there are now specially designed cross-country or 'event' saddles. These saddles are fairly deep-seated with plenty of knee support and fall somewhere between a showjumping and a general-purpose saddle in style. To prevent you from having to invest in both a cross-country and a dressage saddle, some manufacturers have incorporated an adjustable stirrup bar which allows you to move the stirrup bar progressively backwards to accommodate your longer leg position for the dressage phase.

American saddles have also greatly influenced the eventing market in recent times. These saddles have a more open seat with little, if any, knee support, which is supposed to offer more stability, but without restriction. This is all right of course, if you can ride like the Americans and want a saddle that offers minimal support.

Continental manufacturers have also developed saddles for cross-country riding. In the main these are deep-seated, close-contact saddles which incorporate thigh blocks. Some of these blocks are removable which allows for individual preferences for different phases of the event.

Showing

Show saddles have a straight-cut flap which slopes backwards in order to show off as much of the the horse's shoulder as possible. Most have ridged trees, so that they sit low and close

to the horse's back so as not to detract from the horse's top line. They can be very small, so that you hardly see them under the rider, although many are of a normal size for the dimensions of the horse. Some show saddles have full panels, while others only have a half panel to remove bulk from under the rider's leg. They position the rider further back than most saddles, in order to maximize freedom of movement of the forehand. Owing to their flat and often hard seat they do not always give the most comfortable of rides, so you will probably also want a GP saddle for everyday exercise. Always remember a show saddle should also be comfortable for the judge, so you need to choose one that will accommodate a larger or smaller person than yourself – so go for a medium-sized seat. It may not be 'ideal' for you – but if a judge is uncomfortable he is not going to be very impressed.

Racing

It would be quite difficult to confuse a racing saddle with any other design as it has a very distinctive style. The most important feature of a racing saddle is its weight, as this will determine whether or not a weight cloth is necessary. Common to all designs of racing saddle are their flat seats and very forward-cut flaps which allow for the very short stirrup length and forward knee.

Flat-racing saddles are extremely lightweight and offer little security. They can be very uncomfortable and disconcerting for jockeys on flighty thoroughbreds before the off which is why they have been nicknamed 'postage stamp' saddles.

Steeplechase saddles have a little more substance to them, but nevertheless are still quite skimpy compared with riding-saddle standards. Race-exercise saddles have more body to them and therefore provide a little more peace of mind. All racing saddles should be worn with saddle cloths and wither pads as they are so shallow down the gullet that they do not even make a pretence of fitting the horse properly.

Show saddles are designed to show off as much of the horse's shoulder as possible.

Side-Saddles

Not all horses make suitable mounts for side-saddles. Those with a pronounced wither are fine, but the more rounded, flat-withered horse will not be able to prevent the saddle from slipping. Most side-saddles are designed for the rider's legs to be on the near side of the horse. The seat of a side-saddle should be relatively wide and flat, and level from side to side and from front to back. Preferably, it will be covered in doeskin as this provides a non-slip surface. There are two pommels on a side-saddle; one is fixed (called the fixed head), while the other (called the leaping head) is adjustable to accommodate different thigh widths. It is important that you can adjust the side-saddle in this way to gain an optimum fit as this allows you to balance more effectively.

Balancing in a side-saddle that is too big for you is not easy.

The flap on the near side of the saddle is large in order to accommodate your right leg, while the offside flap is usually quite small and unobtrusive. In order to prevent the side-saddle from swinging from side to side as the horse moves, which would cause sores, a balance strap is used which runs down and across the horse's belly. This is used in conjunction with a normal girth, although Fitzwilliam girths are quite popular as they offer added security.

Endurance

While a well-fitting general purpose saddle will suffice for shorter rides, once you start on distances of 60km (40 miles) upwards, you

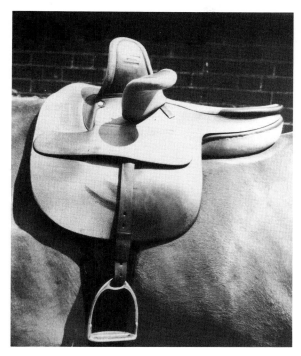

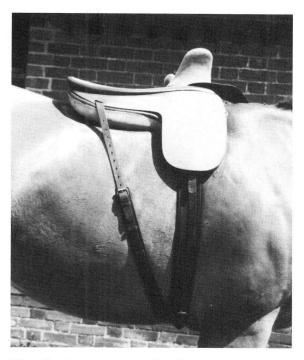

The two pommels: the top one is fixed, while the lower, called the 'leaping head', is adjustable to suit individual thigh size.

The off side, showing smaller flap and balancing strap.

should consider a specialist endurance saddle for both your horse's and your own comfort. There are two basic patterns of endurance saddle, the **Western** and the **English**; but whatever the pattern, the demands remain the same. As your horse must be allowed to go forwards on a free rein, a well-designed endurance saddle will allow your leg to be long, but still allow you to achieve an independent seat. Such a saddle will also provide extra stability over arduous and hilly terrain, while distributing your weight evenly over a large bearing surface on your horse's back, ensuring his comfort.

Long-distance saddles are continually being developed in the quest to reduce pressure points and provide optimum comfort for both horse and rider. Specially designed numnahs are also used under these saddles to prevent friction and offer comfort to the horse while saddled all day.

Western Saddles

There are five main patterns of Western saddle, which can range from anything between 9 and 20.5kg (20 and 45lb) in weight. The heaviest of all is the **ranch saddle**, which is the type most English riders associate with Western riding. It is designed to provide stability when riders are throwing a lasso, and has a low cantle which facilitates the rider jumping down quickly.

The **competition cutting saddle** has a high swell (*see* illustration) and cantle, with a low flat seat. This is in order to 'hold' the rider in position as he or she twists and turns at great speed during a 'cutting' contest.

The **pleasure** or **equitation saddle** is designed to give the rider the most comfort. The seat slopes gently backwards and the set of the swell and cantle is such that the rider can achieve a balanced position, especially as

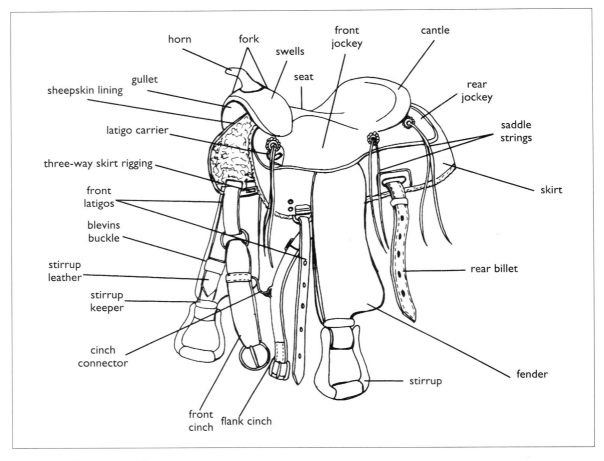

Parts of a Western saddle.

the stirrups are set further under the seat than in other Western saddles, which is more in line with the English position. They are often highly decorated.

Western endurance, or **competition trail saddles** are designed to be as lightweight as possible, yet still hard wearing. Comfort is also a major consideration and the seat is often padded. The fenders are often replaced by thin stirrup leathers, similar to the English type.

Barrel-racing saddles are the most lightweight of the Western saddles. As their name suggests, they are designed for barrel racing and have forward-sloping fenders and stirrups so that the rider can drive his or her legs home to attain a balanced and effective position while performing sharp turns at high speeds. The seat is narrow and compact to secure the rider in place during such manoeuvres.

CONSTRUCTION

While you are probably familiar with the main parts of an English saddle, it is also as well to acquaint yourself with the lesser-known parts, as these will allow you to appreciate the subtleties required for a good fit (*see* illustrations on page 84).

One of the most important parts of any saddle is the tree, upon which it is built. The tree

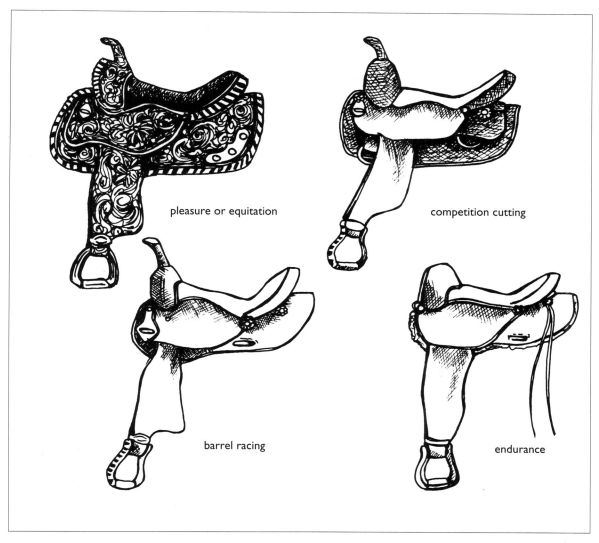

Types of Western saddle.

is the saddle's frame and is hidden from view, so unless you buy a reputable make you will not know how good it is. Most British trees are made from laminated beechwood which is reinforced with metal. Saddle trees come in three widths – narrow, medium and wide – and varying lengths from 35–45.7cm (13⅜–18in) – from pommel to cantle – to suit all sizes of horses. The tree can be rigid, where it allows no movement, or sprung, where it allows a small amount of flexion. Saddles are also made with adjustable trees, which can be altered to fit a range of horses or modified to cope with your horse's changing condition.

TACK TIP

Try to avoid mounting from the ground by pulling yourself up on the cantle of the saddle. This is the quickest way to twist the tree, so use a mounting block instead – a method which is also better for your horse's back.

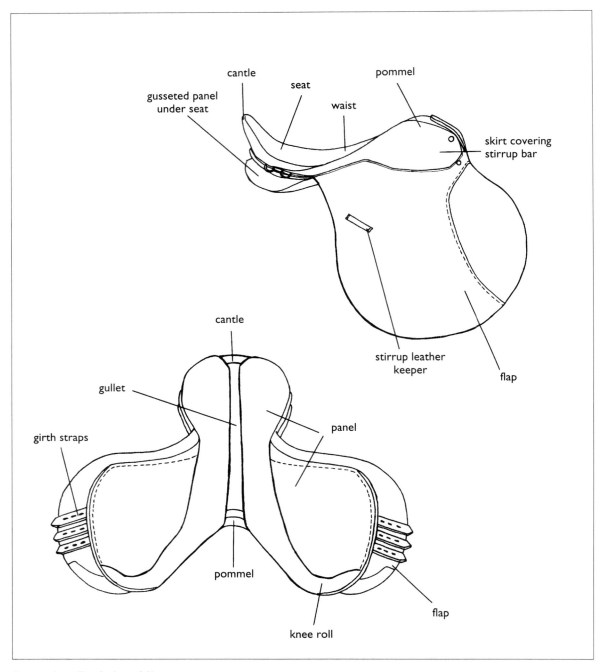

Parts of an English saddle.

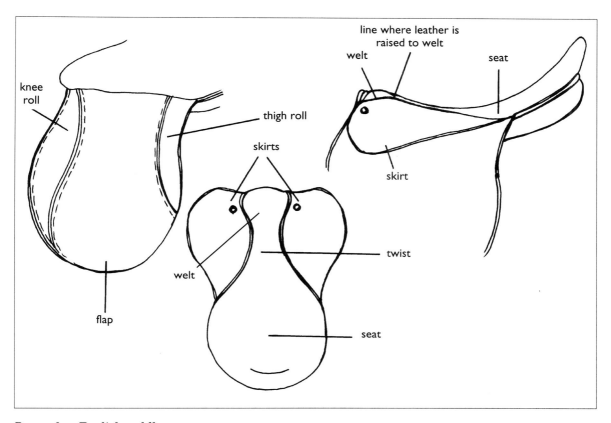

Parts of an English saddle.

Adjustable Trees

Horses, like people, change shape from time to time. If they are in work they will be lean and firm, but if only ridden once a week from grass they may be fat and flabby. Also, an immature three year old may turn into a strapping big five year old and, unavoidably, his saddle will no longer fit. The answer is the adjustable tree which can be incorporated into any saddle but, as with all modern advances, such new ideas are often viewed sceptically. Adjustable trees do operate well: by making a simple adjustment you can make the one saddle fit a range of horses, or make minor adjustments as your horse changes shape. Adjustable trees do add another 20 per cent to the cost of the saddle, so it all depends on whether you consider this to be a valuable investment for your situation.

FITTING

If purchasing a new saddle, it is wise to have a qualified saddler fit it in the first instance. However, as your horse's shape will alter from time to time (when he is in soft condition, his back conformation will be different from when he is lean and fit) constant evaluation of the fit will be required by you. To check the fit of your horse's saddle follow these steps:

1. Stand your horse up on a hard, flat surface. Make sure his back is clean and that he is standing square.
2. Place the saddle gently and smoothly slightly forward of your horse's back and gently slide it backwards until it comes to rest of its own accord. Do not use a numnah under-

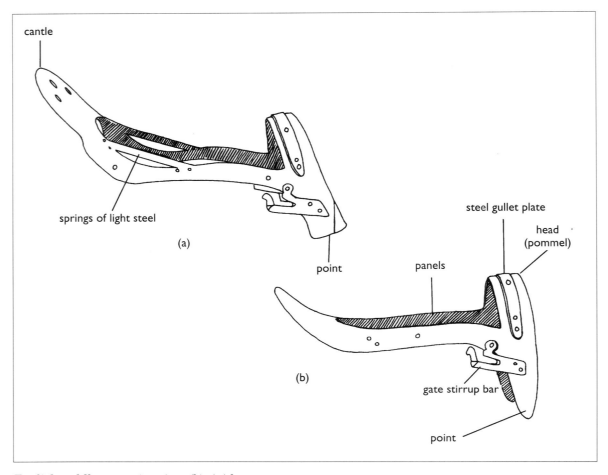

cantle

springs of light steel

(a)

point

panels

steel gullet plate

head
(pommel)

(b)

gate stirrup bar

point

English saddle trees: a) spring; (b) rigid.

neath as this will prevent you from assessing the fit accurately.

3. Do up the girth one hole at a time until the saddle is secure.

4. Stand back and take an overall look. Does it look right? Does it follow the shape of your horse or are there gaps between the panels and his sides? It is often fairly obvious from such an overall look that the saddle does not fit – it simply looks 'wrong.' The cantle should be slightly higher than the pommel as this will ensure you are positioned in the centre of the saddle when riding. If the pommel is higher than the cantle you will tip backwards when riding and, conversely, if the cantle is very

much higher than the pommel you will be tipped forwards. Such a saddle may be designed perfectly well, but simply not for your particular horse.

5. Next, check to see if it fits at the pommel. If the saddle is second-hand you should be able to place three fingers between the lowest point of the pommel and your horse's withers. New saddles will sink a little after use, so allow for four fingers if the saddle is new. The width across the pommel should allow for it to follow the contours of your horse's withers. If it is too wide, the pommel will sink down and rub on the horse's withers; too narrow and your horse's back will be pinched. This is the

Having fitted a saddle, ask yourself if it looks right. Clearly this one does not.

This saddle is so high at the wither that it allows a whole fist to pass through.

structure of the saddle; there can be no alterations – either it fits or it does not!

6.   Now check the cantle. You should be able to place four fingers between your horse's spine and the cantle. Look down the spine: does the gullet completely clear the backbone? Can you see daylight through to the withers?

7.   Next take a look at your horse's shoulders. Do the panels lie snugly against them without hindering movement? Have someone walk your horse on for you; if you can see the muscles bunching up against the panel, movement is being impeded. It may be possible to rectify this by altering the flocking. Ask your saddler about this.

8.   When viewed from behind, the back panels should sit snugly along the horse's back. If there is any point at which the back and panels do not touch, the saddle does not fit. Such a saddle will cause friction points, rubbing and ultimately saddle sores. Again, it may be possible to improve the situation by reflocking

the saddle, but it is far better to get a perfect fit from the start.

9.   If you are satisfied that the saddle appears to fit, mount your horse to check the fit while under your weight. Do not use stirrups as this will alter the distribution of your natural weight and position. While standing still, check the pommel. Can you get two fingers in comfortably? Then check the cantle – can you get three in? Have someone look down the gullet – does it still clear the backbone? Can they still see daylight? Does it look symmetrical from front and rear?

10.   How does it feel? Are you comfortable? Does your horse seem to object at all? Where does the saddle place you – are you sitting upright and in the centre?

11.   Walk, trot and then canter on both reins. Does your horse feel 'normal' and free and easy throughout each pace? Ask your horse to work through properly. Does he seem to object at all?

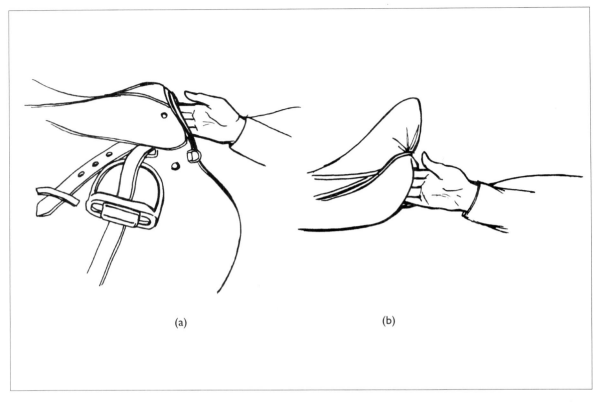

(a) You should be able to place three fingers (four if a new saddle) between the pommel and your horse's withers. (b) You should be able to place four fingers between your horse's spine and the cantle (three once mounted).

TACK TIP

On average, a horse takes 140 steps a minute in trot, so a horse with an ill-fitting saddle will possibly be pinched 4,200 times during a half-hour ride! Responsibility for a good fitting saddle lies with you. Is your horse's saddle a snug fit or a straight-jacket?

High-Tech Assessment

There is a new system of saddle assessment that does not rely on the good 'eye' of a saddler. Developed in the USA, 'Saddle Tech' consists of a pad containing pressure sensors which sits under the saddle. This pad is connected to a computer system which, over every square inch of the panel surface, analyses the amount of pressure exerted by the saddle and rider on the horse's back. Any areas of exceptionally high pressure will show up on the computer display, giving a very real indication of good or poor design and fit.

By utilizing this computerized pressure analysis technology, Philip Richardson has developed the Roe Richardson 'Reactorpanel' APS system. These reactorpanels are designed to improve dramatically the amount and distribution of pressure by doubling the weight-bearing surface. Their fundamental objective is to lower the average pressure under the saddle while the horse is moving, as well as while stationary. These panels are set on multi-positional shock-absorbing mounts; thus by adjusting theses mounts, the Roe Richardson saddle set-up can be adapted to fit most horses.

An ill-fitting saddle could possibly pinch a trotting horse 4,200 times during a half-hour ride – ouch!

The Reactorpanel APS system should:
• Allow a full range of movement, especially in the shoulder.
• Distribute loading evenly under the entire saddle panel area, dramatically reducing the likelihood of saddle sores.
• Ensure a contour-hugging fit, even on a moving horse.
• Increase saddle stability.

Rider Considerations

Next you need to ensure the saddle fits you, the rider:

1.   Obviously, a tall slim person will need a different size and shape of saddle from a stockier, shorter person. The considerations are:

• The size and suitability of the seat.
• The length of the saddle flap.
• The position of the knee and thigh rolls.
• The overall balance.
2.   The size of the seat will be governed by your posterior, and as people come in all shapes and sizes, so do saddles, so you should not have too much trouble in finding one to fit. Common sizes range from 34–46cm (13½–18in), the length being taken from one of the front nailheads on the side of the pommel to the centre of the cantle. The 'twist' of the saddle (*see* illustration) will also govern comfort. Usually the narrower the twist the more comfortable the saddle. This does not mean the gullet is narrow in proportion, however. The seam between the twist and skirt (the welt) should be flush to prevent chafing.

3. Generally the longer the leg the longer the saddle flap needs to be, whatever the type of saddle. The length is governed by your upper leg, all of which should be able to sit on the flap.

4. Do the knee and thigh rolls, if the saddle has them (some types do not), hold your thigh in the right place, so that it sits comfortably between the two?

5. As mentioned before, does the saddle put you in the right position, not tipping you forwards or backwards?

Remember, a saddle is a very important part of riding. A quality one which fits well can improve performance tremendously, while a badly fitting one can cause all sorts of problems.

MATERIALS

Until recently all saddles were made of leather, but in the last few years we have seen synthetic saddlery making an impact on riders. Manufacturers of synthetic saddlery have had to battle against the stigma created by the early gaudy synthetic saddles of inferior design. Unfortunately, there are still a lot of 'synthetic sceptics', but gradually makers of quality synthetic saddles are grinding them down. No serious rider should rule out modern advances, or materials because they are 'different' from what they are used to. Some synthetic saddles are so good that they look like 'real' saddles, but the question is do they perform like them?

The competitive price of synthetic saddles mean the eventer on a tight budget could purchase both a jumping ...

Synthetic saddles have certain advantages over their leather counterparts:
• Most are constructed on an indestructible, moulded polymer tree which means it will not break.
• They are made of durable fabrics which can be easily washed and there is no oiling or saddle soaping to be carried out.
• They have interchangeable, removable girth straps.
• They are much lighter than traditional saddles.
• Most come with many years' guarantee.
• They are cheaper than leather saddles.
• They are non-slip in wet weather.

Where, you may ask, is the catch? While there are these advantages to buying a synthetic saddle, some riders do not like the feel of them, reporting that they cannot get 'close' to their horse during close-contact riding. Also, fitting may be more difficult as many are not flocked in the way a leather saddle is. However, those models which have adjustable trees such as the Thorowgood range, allow you, by simply turning the Allen key provided, to adjust the width of the saddle to fit the changing conditions of your horse. These saddles also have flocked panels which can be restuffed and adjusted in the traditional way.

While synthetic saddles might not suit every rider, they do provide alternatives for those on a budget or with lack of time. They provide a feasible option for a competitive event rider to purchase both a dressage and event saddle for the price of a leather general-purpose one. Another attractive factor is their light weight which makes them easy for children or those with bad backs to carry around,

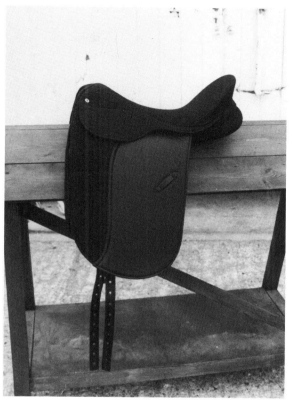

... and dressage saddle for the price of one leather general-purpose one.

and they are also fairly tough so will not be ruined by the odd scrape. They are extremely popular with endurance riders, as they do not slip in wet conditions, a feature which may find favour with any event rider who has had to remount and carry on after a fall in the water. They also find favour with first-time buyers or weekend riders, as well as with people who want a back-up for their expensive leather saddle while carrying out the training of young horses.

6 Saddle Accessories —————

In order to make the best use of your saddle you need to choose the most appropriate accessories for your interests. You need to select the right girth in order to secure your saddle; the right stirrup irons for safety and so on; it is not simply a case of settling for the items that are on the saddle when you look at it in the shop.

LEATHERS

Stirrup irons and leathers are a couple of the very few items of tack where only the rider needs to be considered. When choosing a pair of leathers you should make sure they are strong enough, yet narrow enough to slip through the stirrup eye without having to be forced. Only leathers of the highest quality should be selected, as your life could depend on them.

Children's leathers are obviously narrower than a larger adult's, and widths range from about 1.5–3.2cm (⅝–1¼in). As long as the leather is of good quality it is not necessary to use extra-thick leathers in an attempt to ensure safety. They will prove to be more bulky and could therefore affect comfort and position, doing more harm than good.

Apart from the basic design of leathers, there are also extending leathers and competition leathers. The extending leather is designed for those who have difficulty in mounting, and so only the one used on the mounting side is necessary. A hook and slot attachment, to which a strong piece of webbing is attached at either end, allows the leather to extend for another 15–20cm (6–8in)

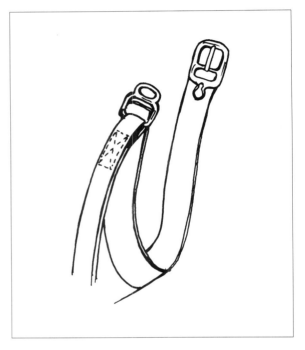

Extending leather.

or so. Once mounted, the slot is simply placed over the hook, and the leather is at the correct length for riding. Always keep a constant check on the webbing and replace immediately at any sign of wear and tear. Should it break while you are trying to mount it will provide a nasty shock.

Competition leathers are a recent innovation. They are strengthened to provide added security when extra pressure is applied. They are basically one single strip of leather which has been split down the centre, thus producing two lengths. A nylon insert is then sandwiched between the two and the leather is then resewn.

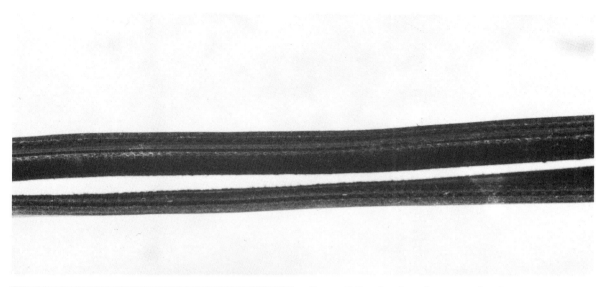

Competition leathers have a nylon insert sandwiched between two leather strips.

> **TACK TIP**
>
> All 'leathers' made of leather will stretch with use and one more so than the other. The near side one is especially prone to this if mounting from the ground, or as a result of putting more pressure in one stirrup than the other during riding, which is common, so it is sensible to alternate them from left to right each time they are removed for cleaning.

STIRRUP IRONS

These should always be made of stainless steel. Other metals have been used, such as nickel, but this has a tendency to bend and break and is therefore not a safe choice. Irons come in a variety of different patterns, each designed with safety or competition in mind.

Stirrup Iron Patterns

Basic pattern
These are the most widely used stirrup iron in everyday riding and they are often referred to

The basic pattern stirrup iron is the most widely used for all activities.

The peacock safety iron is ideal for light adults and children.

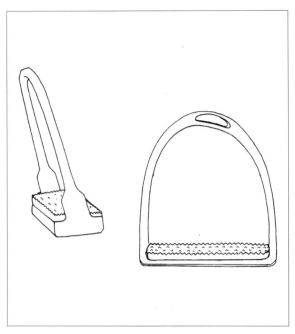

Types of stirrup iron: Kournakoff.

as 'English Hunting Irons'. Providing they are of the right size, they remain the safest choice for almost every purpose, except racing.

Peacock Safety Stirrups
These have a thick rubber belt attached to the bottom of the outside of the iron, by means of a leather loop and stud, to prevent the belt from being lost if it is pulled off. The other end of the belt fixes to a hook at the top of the iron. In the event of a fall, a child or lighter rider's foot will easily be released from the stirrup as the band will simply pull off the hook, whereas such riders may not pull leathers from the stirrup bar in the normal way, due to the light weight. They are only effective if the band is on the *outside* of the foot, so this must be ensured at all times.

The design does have one drawback in that it defies the rule of having a balanced stirrup of the correct weight. The belt side obviously loses weight from the stirrup, which results in it hanging unevenly.

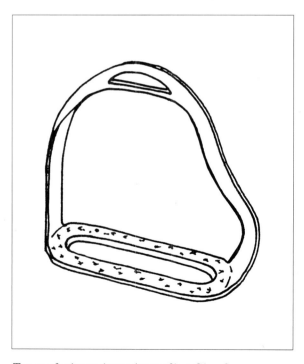

Types of stirrup iron: Australian Simplex.

Kournakoff

This design has an offset eye to the inside, where the leather passes through. The bars of the stirrup slope forwards, and the tread should slope upwards to encourage the toe to be higher than the heel, although this is not always seen. While these irons find favour with those who jump, as they encourage the foot to slope towards the horse and turn the knee in slightly as well, they can be uncomfortable if you are used to the basic pattern, so will need some getting used to.

Australian Simplex

These are also known as bent leg irons as they have a forward bulging bar on the *outside*. As with the peacock stirrups, they are designed so that the foot cannot become trapped in a fall. If you are not satisfied with the basic pattern and are looking for a safety stirrup, then these are certainly worth a try. Be prepared for your feet to slip out quite frequently until you become used to them.

Bent Top

These irons have a bend in the top, sloping forwards and away from the boot. They are especially useful for riders who have a tendency to push the feet well forward in the stirrup as the top of the iron will not put pressure on the front of the ankle, where the basic pattern would. They can also encourage a lowering of the heel.

Turned Eye

These irons have the eye at right angle to the bars, so they lie at right angles to the saddle, and not flat against the horse' sides as with normal irons. They may be of benefit to a rider who constantly loses his or her stirrups, although the problem in this case is more likely to be one of incorrect position than of stirrup design.

Racing Irons

These are very lightweight irons, often made of aluminium. Their shape is that of the basic

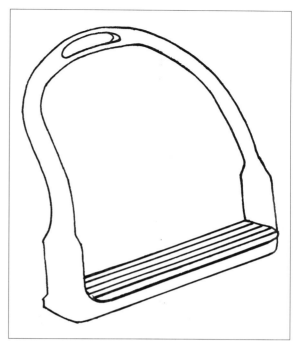

Types of stirrup iron: bent top.

pattern, or they may be slightly rounder. Their sole use lies in flat racing as their weightlessness renders them dangerous for any other purpose.

Size and Weight

Apart from the design, which is a personal choice, the size and weight of the iron needs to be considered. Size is related to the size of your footwear. The irons should be wide enough to allow 1.25cm (½in) either side of your footwear, *not* your foot. Needless to say, the footwear, preferably a proper riding boot (long or short), should have a good heel to prevent the foot from slipping through the iron. When measuring for stirrups, take the measurement across the widest part of your boot sole, remembering that some soles protrude a good few millimetres either side.

The weight of your irons also plays an important part in your safety while riding. Too light an iron will not stay put in the event of a fall, but will follow your foot, which could result in you being dragged.

On no account should you attempt to tie your foot into the stirrup for fear of losing it while competing. If you do experience problems in regaining your stirrups, you could use a piece of plaiting thread tied from the stirrup bar to your spur. This will keep the two together under normal conditions, but will easily snap should you part company with your horse.

> ─── TACK TIP ───
>
> If you use an iron which is too small for your footwear, your foot may become jammed in the stirrup. If you use too large a pair you will be in danger of your foot's slipping right through the stirrup. In either case, you risk being dragged in the event of a fall.

Stirrup Treads

Treads are essential as they provide a non-slip surface for your boot to get a grip on. Most stirrup irons come with either black treads, which have ridges running across them lengthways, or white treads which have rows of raised pimples. The black treads seem to wear more quickly and this is reflected in price as they are cheaper.

Most treads are flat for everyday riding, although you can get ones which are built up on the inside. These are often seen in the dressage arena and sometimes in showjumping, where the rider wants to keep a very close contact with the inside of the leg.

Stirrup Caps

Toe caps or 'Devonshire Boots' are used to prevent the foot from slipping through the stirrups. They are often used in trekking centres, as people on holiday may not have the correct riding footwear. They are also useful for riders who have some form of disability and cannot control their leg position accurately; thus they are still able to ride safely.

STIRRUP BARS

The importance of having the stirrup bar safety catch correctly adjusted cannot be overemphasized. To make this quite clear, the catch at the end of the stirrup bar should always be *down*. If you think of the stirrup bar as simply being one length of metal (which it should be and often is on synthetic saddles) then you will never put it up. Stirrup bar catches often become stiff or rusty, and if they are in the up position will not release the leather if the rider's foot becomes jammed in the stirrup in the event of a fall. This results in the rider being dragged along the ground.

Safety catches on stirrup bars are an annoying little quirk in the making of saddles: they should never be used, but are still fitted to most saddles. Why don't saddlers use plain flat bars without a catch?

Some saddles have adjustable stirrup bars. These can be very useful where you cannot afford the price of two different saddles for dressage and jumping, as they will allow the leg to be placed further forward, or more under your seat as required.

GIRTHS

Girths, although simple pieces of equipment, are nevertheless essential tack items. While their only purpose is to keep the saddle in place, and thus also provide an anchorage point for certain accessories, there are considerations which need to be taken into account when selecting and using them.

Girths come in many different designs and certain ones are often preferred to others for the various disciplines. Appropriate selection may also depend on the horse's conformation, or skin sensitivity. Once fitted they should sit snugly in the sternum groove. Traditionally, girths were made of leather and while this is still popular today, many more materials are now available.

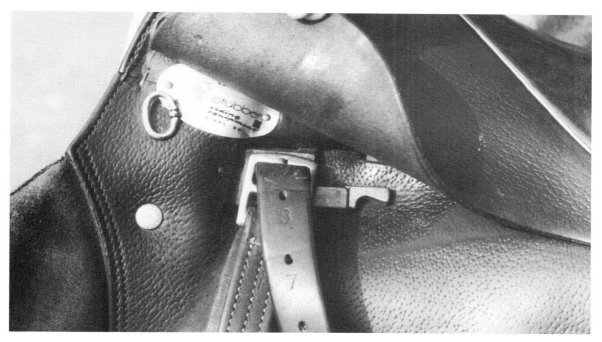

Safety catches on stirrup bars should always be down.

Leather Girths

Leather girths are strong and it is rare to have one snap unless it has been very badly maintained. However, they do have their drawbacks. Firstly, they do not allow air to circulate and so the horse sweats underneath them during exercise. Secondly, they have very little give (unless they have elastic inserts) and so are not as comfortable for the horse as other materials in use. The three most common designs are the Balding pattern, the Atherstone pattern and the three-fold.

Balding pattern
This is one of the most popular designs. About 25.5cm (10in) from the buckles on each side it splits into three, with the two outside lengths being slightly narrower than the middle one. These outside strips are crossed over each other, which results in the girth being narrower behind the horse's elbow. Underneath the horse's belly, the strips are stitched to a short length of leather to provide a flat surface. It is used to prevent rubbing and chafing behind the elbow which in turn prevents girth galls. However, one drawback is that the pressure is unevenly spread.

Atherstone pattern
This girth also narrows behind the elbow but is a single length of leather which has been suitably shaped. It is usually seen in leather, but the pattern has been adapted for use with other materials. It often has elastic inserts on one side, but the better design has these inserts on both sides to balance the girth at each end. The idea is that the girth 'gives' a little in accordance with the horse's movement and allows for the expanding lungs when extra effort is being given and so offers a little more comfort. If the girth only has one elastic insert, ensure it is on the off side to prevent overtightening. At the very first sign of the elastic's fraying a new insert must be fitted, or the girth changed altogether.

97

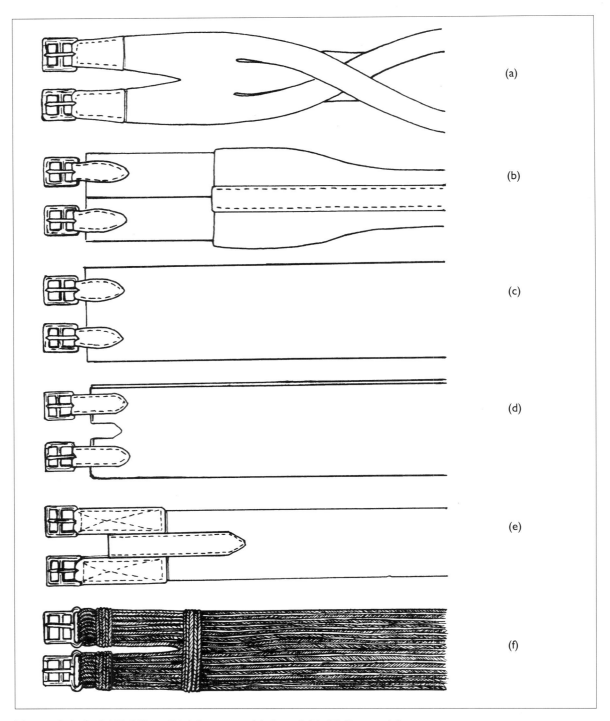

Types of girth: (a) Balding; (b) Atherstone; (c) three-fold; (d) Lampwick;
(e) foam-padded cotton; (f) German cordstring.

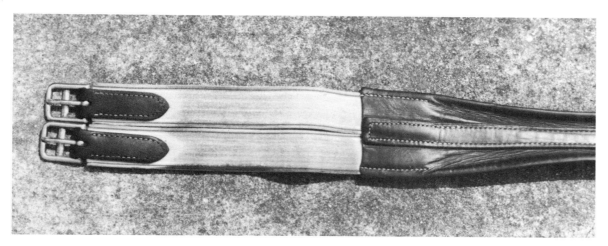

The Atherstone girth often has elastic inserts to provide extra 'give'.

Three-fold

This is another leather pattern, usually made of baghide. As its name suggests, it is folded three times, leaving one edge smooth and rolled and one edge open. An oiled piece of fabric is placed inside the folds to keep the leather supple. When fitted, the rolled edge should face the horse's elbow as the open edge would pinch. This pattern does not wear as well as other leather girths and often starts to curve backwards out of shape under the horse's belly.

Leather Alternatives

Girths which are the most practical for everyday use are those which are made of permeable or absorbent materials. They provide coolness in summer or when working hard, as the sweat is permitted to evaporate through the girth. Most girths which use such materials are made in simple, single-length designs.

Lampwick

Until a few years ago these were the most widely used of the non-leather girths. They are made of tubular wick which is very soft and is unlikely to cause chafing, so they are the most suitable choice for horses with sensitive skins.

Foam-padded Cotton

These are the market leaders in non-leather girths, and although most people will associated them with the name 'Cottage Craft', there are other manufacturers. They are extremely easy to keep clean as they can be machine washed, which, added to their natural softness, makes them ideal for any horse prone to girth galls.

German Cordstring

These are made up of thick cotton cords which are held together by evenly spaced crossweave panels. They are quite wide, so provide a wide, even bearing surface. Their most useful application is in holding saddles in place on horses with hairy coats, as the individual strands grip the coat. They are also ideal for flat-withered or rather round horses as they can prevent the saddle from drifting back. It is important to pull each of the horse's forelegs forward once the girth is tightened to ensure that all the strands are lying flat against the skin, otherwise pinching will occur. It is also important to keep them scrupulously clean by soaking in a bucket, before rinsing.

Nylon String

This is an extremely poor relation to the German cordstring and has none of its attributes.

The girth will pinch the skin quite readily and, having become wet with sweat, it dries to leave a harsh, abrasive surface rubbing next to the horse's skin.

Fitzwilliam

This girth enables all three girth straps to be used and is therefore used where absolute security is required. It comprises two lengths of leather: one wide band, and a further narrower band which sits on top of this. The wide band is done up to the girth straps in the normal way, utilizing the two outside straps. The narrower band is slightly shorter than the wide band, and this does up on the middle girth strap, but will be a few holes lower. Obviously if one band was to give, then the saddle would still be held in place by the other. It is still used quite a lot on side-saddles, as these put more strain on the girth than other astride models.

Humane

This can be of threefold design or made of web. The length of the girth is as any other, but at each end of the belly strap there is a slotted link, through which a sliding strap with a buckle on each end passes. This allows the strap to move slightly in accordance with the horse's movements and therefore performs the same function as the elastic girth inserts, but with a little more security.

Short Dressage

There are various types of these, but the one almost universally used is the Lonsdale girth. It is designed for use on dressage saddles which have only two, extended girth straps. This enables the buckles to be secured out of the way of the rider's thigh, which is very important for close-contact riding. When buying a Lonsdale girth, ensure you choose one that has the buckles at least 5cm (2in) from the top of the girth. This will ensure there is adequate protection from the buckles which would otherwise rub and pinch the horse's sides.

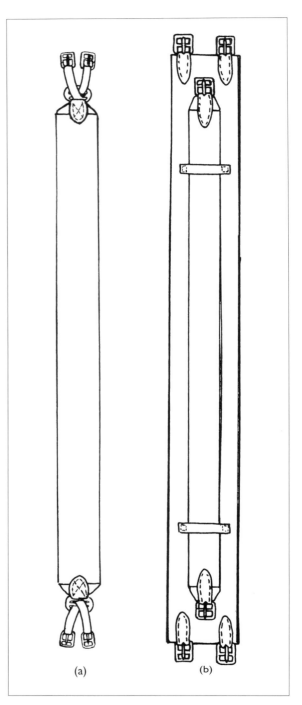

(a) (b)

Types of girth continued: (a) humane;
(b) Fitzwilliam.

Length and Width

A girth should do up on equal holes either side of the saddle, so you do need to buy a girth of the correct size to achieve this. When initially fitting it should do up on the middle holes, allowing for tightening and loosening as required. A girth that does up midway at each side will also distribute pressure more evenly.

Most girths come in standard widths of between 9 and 11.5cm (3½ and 4½in) wide. Usually, for reasons of strength, the longer the girth the wider it is, unless it is a particular design such as the Lonsdale girth which is short but wide, or an overgirth which is long and narrow. It is common sense that for comfort, the small pony requires a narrower girth

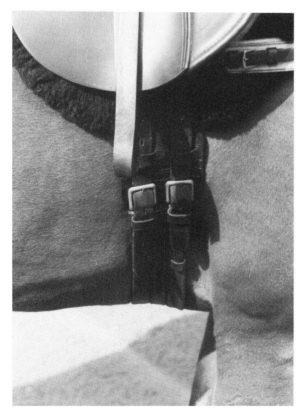

A good type of Lonsdale girth which has buckle protectors.

than the 17hh. hunter. However, every girth needs to be wide enough to spread the pressure without being too restrictive.

Problems
The biggest problem arising from the use of girths is the girth gall, most often caused by sweat or by working horses in 'soft' condition. To harden up the skin when using leather girths, surgical spirit or salt water can be applied daily. To protect the horse while the skin is hardening, a sheepskin girth sleeve can be used.

The girth buckles rubbing against the saddle flap can also cause some problems, namely wearing and marking of the leather. To prevent this, 'girth safes', or buckle protectors as they are often referred to, can be fitted to the girth straps on each side of the saddle.

OVERGIRTHS

An overgirth is used as an added security measure when jumping or riding across country. It is made of strong webbing and is put on over the top of the saddle and lies along the girth under the horse's belly, thus completely encircling the saddle. Should the ordinary girth give, the overgirth will prevent the saddle from slipping off. Most have an elastic insert to provide a little bit of give during strenuous exercise.

Overgirths are sometimes known as jumping surcingles, although this is not to be confused with an ordinary surcingle which holds rugs in place and is made in many unpadded fabrics.

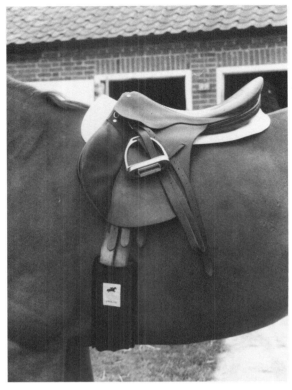

To protect the skin of a sensitive horse, a girth sleeve (this one is made of gel) can be used.

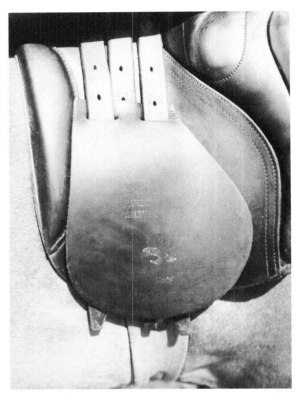

A good type of girth safe which offers maximum protection from buckles as it does not have to be constantly pulled down over the buckles.

TACK TIP

When buying an overgirth make sure you choose one with plenty of tabs to hold the end of the strap in place. As an overgirth does up under the horse's belly, a trailing strap could cause annoyance or, worse, an accident.

BREASTPLATES

The purpose of a breastplate is to prevent the saddle from slipping backwards, and there are two basic types: the hunting style and the racing style (also known as breastgirths). It is largely a matter of personal choice which you use, but the hunting type is more versatile as martingale attachments can be fitted.

Hunting Style

Breastplates are often used on horses being ridden in cross-country events as a precaution in case the saddle slips backwards when the horse gives maximum effort over a jump. At the point of take-off and while in motion over the fence his muscles will be taut, which makes the saddle and girth slack and therefore vulnerable to slipping at such moments. Some horses have conformation faults, such as being 'herring gutted', which means the saddle is likely to work its way backwards. In such cases the use of a breastplate is a sensible safety measure whenever the horse is being ridden.

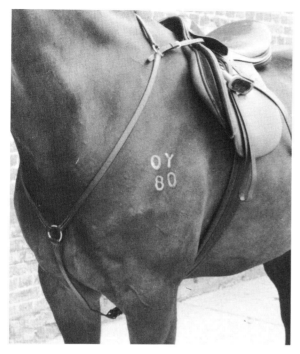

A hunting-style breastplate with breast ring for martingale attachments.

Fit

A breastplate has a neck strap which attaches by means of a loop to the girth, as with a martingale. The neckstrap and girth loop are both fixed to a breast ring, to which the martingale attachments can be fixed. Well-made designs have a 'leather safe' behind this ring to prevent it from rubbing the chest. Two straps of leather then affix to rings on the breastplate forward of the withers, which run to the saddle and attach to its D-rings by straps and buckles on either side of the horse, thus preventing the saddle from moving backwards. A breastplate should allow a hand's width between it and the horse's neck and the girth loop should not hang lower than 10cm (4in) under the horse's chest.

A breastplate can be stout or fine depending on the type of horse and the intended activity. A hunter will suit a strong, thick design, whereas an Arab will look better in a finer one.

Breastplates have one drawback in that they can become tight around the horse's forelegs and chest in their attempt to hold the saddle forwards if it does start to work its way backwards. It is pointless to loosen the breastplate to prevent this happening as it will then not do its job. Where this does occur, other measures such as using a string girth should also be taken.

Racing Style (Breastgirths)

Racehorses often wear breastgirths as their saddles are so light that they need to be firmly anchored. Also, the saddles sometimes lack the D-rings required for attaching a breastplate.

Unlike a breastplate, the breastgirth does not attach to the girth under the horse's forelegs, but to the girth on either side of the saddle. A wither strap sits over the horse's neck which runs down on either side of the horse's neck to a wide breaststrap which is made of webbing, elastic or leather. This sits just above the points of the horse's shoulders. Two leather straps then run from this to the girth which are done up by means of buckles around the girth under the saddle flaps. The most common breastgirth is known as the 'Aintree' breastgirth. This is often covered in a roll of sheepskin to prevent chafing. The polo pattern breastgirth is also quite common. It has a slot or sewn leather loop on the breaststrap to which a martingale attachment can be fitted. The elastic type is used where a certain amount of give is required.

CRUPPERS

In contrast to breastplates, cruppers are used to prevent a saddle from coming forwards. A smooth, padded loop of leather fixes over the dock and a long strap runs from this to a ring at the rear of the saddle in the centre, or more occasionally through the centre gullet to a ring on the front of the saddle; or it splits into

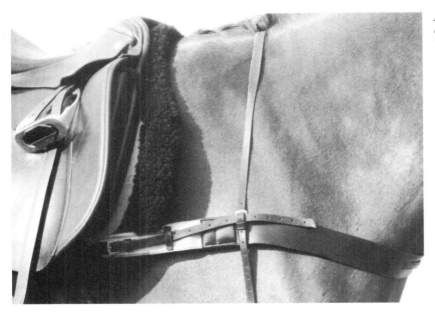

A strong breastgirth with elastic inserts to allow some 'give'.

Breastgirths are invaluable where you need to prevent a saddle from slipping, but also want to use an independently fitted martingale.

two and fixes to the D-rings on either side of the saddle. The strap is tightened until there is no slack, but not so that it pulls on the dock. The padded loop may also have buckles on either side so that you can tighten the loop from the rear, rather than having to lean over the horse's back. This is useful when dealing with young horses. The padded loop is often stuffed with linseed, as this seeps a little oil and keeps the leather supple and smooth. A crupper is always used on driving horses, but it is also useful for fat little ponies with little wither whose saddles often drift forwards. They have prevented many a young child from tipping off over their pony's neck because the saddle has worked forward and slipped around to his chest. They are also useful on young horses at their start of their ridden education as they secure valuable tack in place should the horse display any high jinks!

NUMNAHS AND SADDLE CLOTHS

Most people use numnahs under the saddle without really thinking why they do so. The most common reason for use is that numnahs are associated with comfort for the horse. While some horses do seem to go better when wearing numnahs, they should not be used as standard, unless they are needed. The worst reason for using a numnah is to protect the back of a horse wearing an ill-fitting saddle. The effect of this is rather like trying to wear a thick pair of socks in order to counteract the pinching effect of a pair of shoes that is too tight for you! An ill-fitting saddle must be replaced, not disguised. Other reasons for not using numnahs include:

• Overheating. Thick numnahs can cause the horse to heat up under the saddle. There is no release for this heat, because the numnah provides an insulating layer between saddle and skin, and so the back may become tender and sore.
• Bulk. Numnahs provide unnecessary bulk between you and your horse, when the aim should be to bring you both closer together. The further away you sit from your horse, the less effectively your seat aids will be transmitted.
• Wetness. Numnahs soon become soaked with sweat, which is uncomfortable for the

horse. This wet layer of sweat gradually dries to leave an encrusted layer of grime which rubs away at the horse's skin. This causes chafing and irritation which can lead to a sore back and skin disease.
• Sliding. Many numnahs slide back and pucker up when in use, which must be extremely uncomfortable for the horse.

There are cases where the use of a numnah is advantageous, but it must be stressed that a numnah is valuable only if there is a good reason for its employment. That your horse genuinely goes better when wearing a numnah is a valid reason, but make sure this is not just imagination on your part. Putting a light saddle cloth under the saddle of a hairy horse is also fine, as this will not have any effect upon fit and will protect the panels from excessive grease and dirt. A numnah can also be of benefit where a horse has a saddle sore caused by the wearing of a poorly fitting saddle. You must, of course, change the saddle to one that fits well, but because saddle sores can take some time to heal you may need to look for a way to continue riding. Take a numnah made of dense material and cut out a hole at the place corresponding with the site of the sore. The thickness of the surrounding material will keep the saddle away from the sore, thus preventing contact and further rubbing. You should then be able to ride the horse without causing him any pain. However, as soon as the sore is healed, the numnah should be dispensed with.

If you are going to use a numnah, take note of the following guidelines:
• Make sure the numnah is the correct shape for your horse's back. Has he got high withers, or very low ones? Such factors need to be considered when selecting the most suitable cut over the wither area.
• Make sure the numnah is the right shape for your saddle. Numnahs come in all the shapes of the various saddles, or you can buy straight ones that extend right over the back.
• Make sure they are of uniform depth. Some

poor designs have padded edges, which if they sit under the saddle will cause pressure points.

• Make sure you pull the numnah well up into the gullet of the saddle so that it does not press on your horse's withers or spine. Check this again after doing up the girth.

• Make sure you keep the numnah scrupulously clean and never put a wet or dirty numnah back on a horse.

• If the numnah constantly puckers up under the saddle, this is a sign of the saddle panels not fitting snugly against the horse's skin. Check the fit of the saddle.

Design and Materials

Numnahs are made in a variety of materials, thicknesses, colours and designs, ranging from the traditional sheepskin ones to the red-and-white striped, modern synthetic types. When choosing a numnah, consider the following:

• What purpose it will be serving.
• How much time you have to care for it. A sheepskin one will need to be cared for by hand, while most synthetics can be put in the washing machine.
• The shape and size of your saddle. Numnahs come in all shapes and three common sizes: pony, cob and full size.

Some have padded sheepskin over the withers, while others have a double cut-out section over the spine area, but only a thin panel section. In theory, this is in order to offer padding along the spine, but remove bulk from under your leg. In practice, the saddle should not be interfering with the spine, so this padding simply causes uneven pressure.

Specialist Numnahs

While it can be said that during normal riding there is little call for the employment of a numnah, it may be beneficial for use on high-

Make sure any numnah used is pulled well up into the gullet of the saddle.

performance horses where it is desirable to reduce impact when jumping, or to absorb sheer forces during close-contact riding. However, no ordinary numnah will do, and in response to such demands specialist types have been made, which come in various materials and designs.

Poly Pads
These are a type of numnah designed to disperse pressure points and thus prevent back problems. They are used extensively by competition riders, especially of high-performance horses, in order to provide a cushioning effect when jumping, thus acting as a shock absorber to the rider landing awkwardly. They require no straps or loops for a secure fit and

Poly pads are a type of numnah designed to disperse pressure points and are very popular with event riders.

do not drift back, however much the horse is exerting himself. When correctly pulled up into the gullet, airflow is maintained along the spine, thus also preventing overheating.

Nuu-Med

These numnahs are recommended by vets and are designed to relieve pressure, absorb moisture, reduce heat build-up and eliminate friction – all the things which other numnahs tend not to do. During an independent trial they were found to be the best type for a horse who does seem to appreciate the use of a numnah, or those whose skin is sensitive under the saddle area. Although they are made of British wool, they are machine washable so there is no excuse for them to be dirty.

Gel Pads

Gel pads have been available for the last decade or so, and while they are effective at preventing pressure sores under the saddle area, they do have a reputation for being fairly heavy, which prevents air flow and results in the horse overheating and sweating profusely under the saddle. As with most things, whenever there are problems, new and better

products are designed to overcome them. One such product that has favourably superseded the old gels is the Prolite gel. It is lightweight and has tremendous absorbing properties, but the most important property of Prolite is its ability to absorb sheer force. A great amount of sheer force can exist under a saddle, especially during close-contact riding such as dressage. It is essential to absorb sheer force in order to eliminate the risk of soft-tissue injury, and in such circumstances the Prolite gel pads are simply the best. They are 80 per cent lighter than traditional gels, but maintain the same degree of impact and sheer force absorption. They do not absorb liquid, and in order to wick any sweat away from the back they are perforated at strategic points.

Another beneficial feature is that they are reversible, so if out riding for the day you can turn them over during a break, to provide a nice clean surface for the horse's back.

Seatsavers or 'People' Numnahs

These are designed purely for rider comfort. They are either made of thick sheepskin, real or artificial, or of foam covered in suede, and simply fit over the top of the saddle, providing

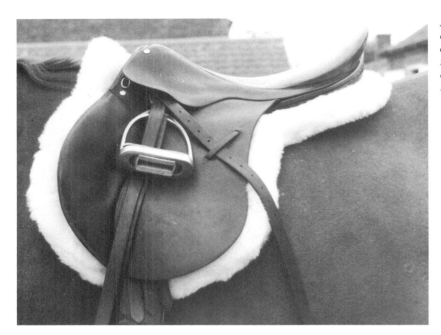

Nuu-Med numnahs are designed to absorb moisture, eliminate friction and reduce heat build-up. This one is the ideal shape for this saddle.

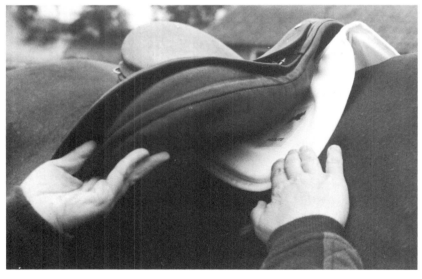

A half-panel Prolite gel pad, which is lightweight and has tremendous absorbing qualities.

a 'cushion'. This may help the rider who becomes sore when riding for long periods as they are designed to prevent chafing and cushion the pelvic bones. A special visco-elastic foam, which was developed by the US Air Force in order to absorb the shock of seat ejec-tion, has been utilized in one particular seat saver. It is claimed that this material allows the rider to absorb some of the upward propulsion of horses with powerful quarters. They are also said to help combat the concussive effects of riding for riders with bad backs.

7 Driving Harness

A set of single harness can have about 40 parts to it!

A set of single driving harness can have about forty parts to it, so unless you know how to put it all together you can get into quite a tangle! Unlike a bridle, it is not easy to work out where all the bits and pieces go, so it is best to have someone experienced show you how to do it. Having put it all together you then have to fit it to the horse, which can be even more of a task. If you are new to driving you will soon learn that the easiest part about the activity is the driving itself. However, do not despair! With a little patience and a lot of practice you will soon be assembling and fitting a harness within minutes.

As with all ridden tack, styles and materials can vary enormously, although the type chosen does need to be suitable for the size of the horse, the type of vehicle to be used, and

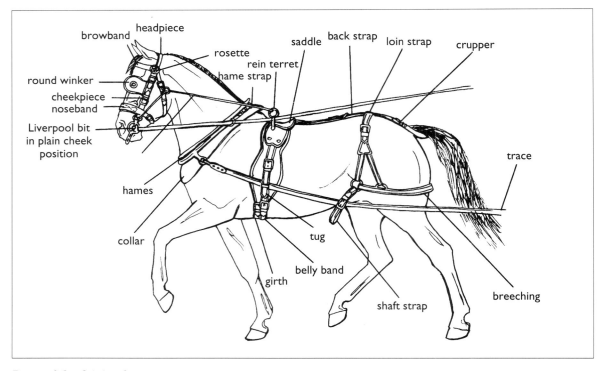

Parts of the driving harness.

the type of driving undertaken. For example, a synthetic harness would not be appropriate for a private driving class but it is totally suitable for everyday exercise and will prevent the hours of cleaning that are a necessary part of using a leather harness.

PARTS OF THE HARNESS

Driving Bridle

This differs from a riding bridle in many respects. Firstly, it has blinkers sewn into the cheekpieces. Their purpose is to prevent the horse from being distracted by things alongside, or behind him, such as the vehicle's wheels or a flapping road sign. They will also prevent the tip of the whip from accidentally flicking into his eyes. Blinkers come in many different styles including round,

square, hatchet and D-shaped ones as well as half-cup blinkers. They should fit snugly to the face, without putting any pressure on the eyes, or interfering with the horse's vision. They are supported by two blinker stays, which buckle on to the headpiece and are adjustable for individual fit.

The cheekpieces themselves have buckles at both top and bottom, with the noseband slipping through them (or the cheekpieces slipping through keepers in the noseband), resembling an in-hand bridle. The browband and throatlash complete the driving bridle and are similar to those found on riding bridles, but usually of a thicker width. Some bridles may also have a face-drop suspended from the centre of the headpiece, which lies on the forehead between the eyes and is purely ornamental. There are other types of driving bridle but this is the type most commonly used for private, single driving. They are sometimes seen in patent leather as well as normal leather.

Driving Bits

There are various driving bits in use, most being curb bits. However, the contact taken with them through the reins does need to be as sensitive, if not more so than when riding, as there are no other physical aids to back them up. If you constantly pull on the mouth of a driving horse he soon learns to pull back even more, and only one of you is going to win a battle of strength!

The bits most frequently used are:

Wilson Snaffle
This is the same four-ring bit as described in Chapter 3, but it is fitted in a different way. The cheekpiece is always attached to the unattached ring. The reins are also attached to this ring but take in the outer ring between the buckle as well. In cases where a more severe bit is needed, the reins are attached to the fixed ring only, bringing in the pinching action, as for ridden horses (*see* Chapter 2). Used in the milder way it is very useful for a horse which dislikes a curb, and is often used for exercise. However, a curb bit is more usual in the show ring as it looks more attractive.

Liverpool Curb
This is the most popular driving bit in use today. It is similar to a Pelham, although only one rein is used, but in various positions as desired. It can have swivel or fixed cheeks of

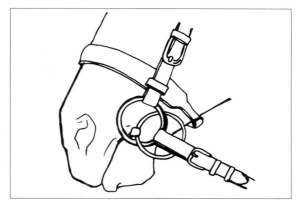

Correct fitting of the Wilson snaffle for driving.

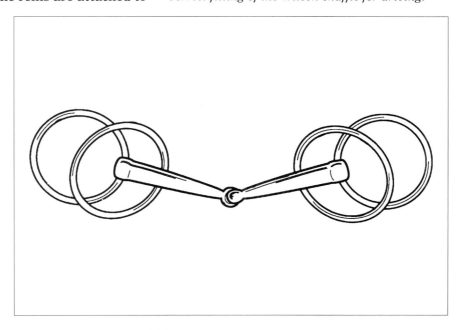

Wilson snaffle.

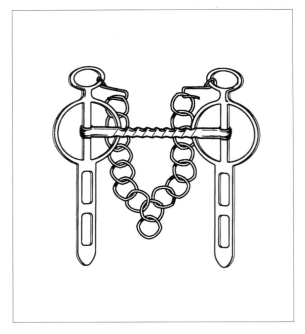

Liverpool bit.

Elbow curb illustration

Elbow curb.

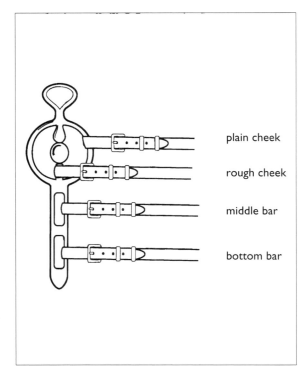

plain cheek

rough cheek

middle bar

bottom bar

The various rein positions.

varying lengths, and has a straight bar mouthpiece, of which one side is serrated. Sometimes a port is incorporated in order to accommodate the tongue, or to prevent the horse from getting his tongue over the bit. Where the rein is attached to the bit-ring (known as the plain cheek position) there is no curb action, and the bit acts like any other straight-bar snaffle. However, as the rein travels down the bit in three more possible positions, the leverage, and thus severity, increases. The mouthpiece should be fitted so that the serrated edge points away from the bars, and the curb-chain so adjusted that it comes into action when the bit-cheeks are at about a 45-degree angle from the mouth when in the lower rein positions.

Elbow Curb
This is similar in action to the Liverpool bit, but has its lower shaft angled backwards away from the mouth. This is to prevent a horse from grabbing hold of it and thus being out of the driver's control.

Buxton Curb

At first glance this looks a rather severe bit, but in truth it is no more so than the Liverpool bit. In fact, its action and use are the same as the Liverpool bit, and it is simply a more ornate design used in the show ring, predominantly on pairs or teams.

Neck Collar

There are various types of collar, depending on the type of horse and vehicle. The neck collar fits around the horse's neck and chest, sitting just in front of his shoulder. It is oval in shape, well padded and covered in leather. A full neck collar distributes the draught weight of the vehicle more evenly over the horse's shoulder and as it is the sole means of the horse propelling the vehicle forward, it is crucial that it is of the correct size and properly fitted. As with saddles, this type of collar may be narrow, medium or wide fitting and should

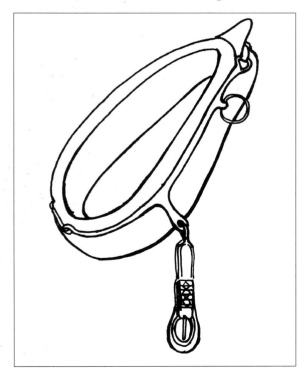

Full neck collar.

initially be fitted by an expert. Considerations such as flat panels to provide a wide-bearing surface are equally as important as with saddle fitting.

A collar is always put on upside down, widest part uppermost, to accommodate the widest part of the horse's head. It is then swivelled round so that the widest part sits above the chest. To ensure a correct fit, make sure you can place your hand between the horse's windpipe and the bottom of the collar.

TACK TIP

As with saddles, once a horse is fitter and more muscled up a different size of collar may be needed, so keep a constant check on correct fit.

Hames

These are the steel branches which lie in the groove between the fore- and afterwale (front and rear section of the collar). They are secured in place by means of leather hame straps, or chains at the top and bottom of the collar. About a quarter of the way down from the top of the hame a fixed or swivelling rein terret is attached, with a tug arm lying about two-thirds of the way down the hame. The traces are attached to this tug arm, or draught pull as it is known, either by being sewn on to a ring attached to it, or by way of a hame tug.

Breast Collar

A breast collar is much lighter, and less expensive, than a full collar. However, its one drawback is that the bearing surface is much narrower and thus the pressure from pulling the vehicle is more intense over this limited area. It is similar in style to a riding breastgirth, but far sturdier. It fits in much the same way as a breastgirth; make sure it sits above the points of the shoulder, but not so that it affects the windpipe. The rein terrets are attached to the neckstrap which sits just in front of the

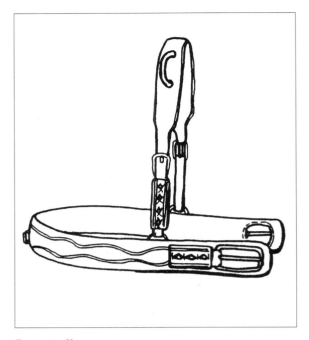

Breast collar.

On top of the driving saddle are two terrets through which the reins pass. Here, two sets of reins are used so that a novice can learn how to drive, but an experienced driver can take charge if necessary.

withers, the traces being attached to solid, strong buckles at the end of the breast collar.

False Martingale

A false martingale is a feature on many sets of harness and it runs from the collar to the girth. It has no effect on the reins or the bridle, as with riding martingales. When it is attached to the D-ring on the underside of a breast collar it is purely a decorative feature. However, when it buckles around the collar and hames it helps to prevent the collar from riding up and interfering with the windpipe.

Driving Saddle

This is the part of the harness which sits on the horse's back, just behind the withers. Its purpose is to take a small proportion of the weight of the vehicle and to help balance the load. The saddle should be fitted carefully ensuring no pressure is put on to the spine. On the top of the saddle there are two terrets through which the reins pass, and in front in the centre of these is a hook to which an overcheck or bearing rein is attached. At the back of the saddle there is a D-ring to which the crupper is attached. The saddle is secured by means of a girth in the usual way.

A back band is a long leather strap with a buckle on one end, or it may be two straps, one with holes in each end and one with a buckle at each end. It is threaded through a channel in the saddle and has tugs attached which lie about two-thirds of the way down the horse's sides. These tugs are strong leather rings, through which the shafts of the vehicle pass. The back band then sits on top of the girth and passes through a girth loop, doing up with one buckle under the belly, or with two on either side. It is not done up as tightly as a girth, as

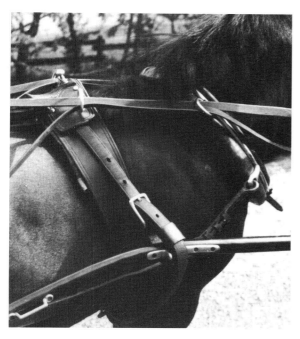

The back band supports the tugs, through which the shafts run.

together with the tugs its only purpose is to prevent the shafts from rising up.

Driving Pad

This serves the same purpose as the saddle, but is much lighter. It has no back band or tugs attached as its function is to carry the tug buckle (to which the traces are attached) on pair harness.

Breeching

This is a strong, wide band which passes around the horse's quarters, midway between the base of the tail and the hocks. Its function is to enable the horse to take the weight of the vehicles on his quarters when travelling downhill, or backing up, although the breaks of the driving vehicle should of course be applied to minimize the weight.

There are two types of breeching: full and false. Full breeching is like a breastgirth in reverse, with a loin strap passing up over the loins and through the crupper backstrap. A further short breeching strap with a buckle is fixed to the end rings of the breeching, which then attach to D-rings on the shafts, thus supporting them. False breeching is simply a stout length of leather to which the short breeching straps are applied and fixed to the shafts as before. It does not attach to the horse, but prevents the vehicle from running forwards.

Driving Crupper

This is a padded loop of leather, which fits around the root of the tail. It may have buckles so that it can be fitted around the tail and individually adjusted, or it may be a continuous oval of leather through which the tail has to be passed. It attaches to the pad or saddle by means of a crupper backstrap, through which the breeching may be secured.

Bearing Reins and Overchecks

These are designed to keep the horse's head up, but must be used in conjunction with a bridoon snaffle, so the horse needs to be fitted with a double bridle. In simple terms, they pass from the hook on the saddle, through the headpiece rings, and are then clipped on to the bit. There are variations, but as bearing reins are seldom used nowadays, there is little point in lengthy explanations.

Traces

Traces are the parts of the harness that actually attach the horse to the vehicle. They are made of multiple layers of leather, stitched together with as many as three or four rows of stitching. The length of the traces will dictate how close the horse is to the vehicle. Ideally he wants to be close to the vehicle, but not so close that his quarters could come into contact with the footboard.

You might think a set of single harness is enough to clean, but it is nothing compared with the type of harness worn by draught animals in show.

Reins

These are simply long lengths of leather about 2.5cm (1in) thick. They may have a buckle at the end to fasten the two together, but many drivers prefer to keep the reins separate to prevent anything from getting caught up in them in an emergency. They usually attach to the bit by means of buckle fastenings as these are easier to adjust when on the bit.

STEP-BY-STEP FITTING

1.   Put on the collar ensuring it fits snugly in front of the shoulder.
2.   Fit the hames into the grooves of the collar and fasten the hame strap.
3.   Place the saddle on the horse's back.
4.   Fit the crupper.
5.   Put the breeching in place.
6.   Do up the girth, remembering to put it through the martingale loop if using one.
7.   Do up the back band.
8.   Put the reins through the terrets on the saddle and collar rings.
9.   Put on the bridle.
10.   Attach the reins.
11.   Draw up the vehicle and slot the shafts through the tugs.
12.   Slip the traces under the back band and attach at the correct distance to the vehicle.
13.   Re-adjust the back band to secure the shafts as necessary.
14.   Attach the breeching straps around the shafts to the D-rings.
15.   Happy Driving!

TACK TIP

Fixing the hame strap is most important. If it were to come loose or break, the horse would continue without the vehicle!

116

8 In-Hand Training Equipment

Two lunge reins can be used for long-reining.

LUNGEING AND LONG-REINING EQUIPMENT

The equipment used for lungeing and long-reining is the same, except when long-reining you use two reins instead of one. The various items needed to lunge safely are:

1. A lungeing cavesson.
2. A lungeing rein with swivel hook.
3. A snaffle bridle (*see* Chapter 1).
4. A lungeing roller with attached breast-girth, or a saddle with stirrups removed.
5. A wither pad if using a roller.
6. A lungeing whip.
7. Fore and hind protective boots (*see* Chapter 9).
8. Side-reins (optional, *see* Chapter 4).
9. Mouthing bit.
10. A crupper (optional, *see* Chapter 6).

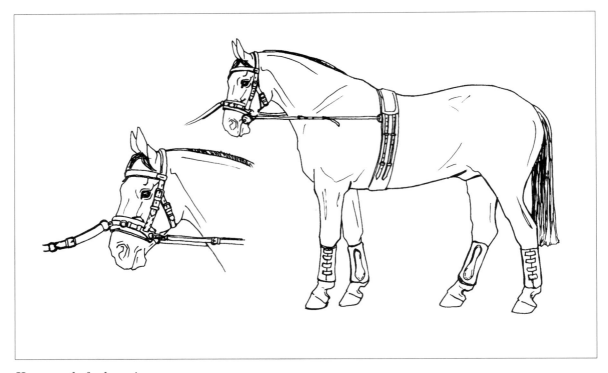

Horse ready for lungeing.

The Lungeing Cavesson

The lungeing cavesson is a most essential piece of in-hand training equipment, used for lungeing and long-reining. It must be made of strong materials as it may take a great amount of force from young horses playing about. There are various designs, some made of web, others of stout leather. The most important criteria are that the cavesson fits snugly, is lightweight but well padded to prevent chafing and is secure, to prevent it from slipping around the face and catching the horse's eye when force is applied to the lunge rein. This is a common hazard of a poorly made cavesson, or one which is too large for the horse's head.

The most common designs are the **Orssich** and **Wels** patterns. The Orssich pattern has three swivel rings on the padded nosepiece: the middle ring is used for lungeing and the

two side rings, known as driving rings, are used for long-reining or 'driving' training. A browband is a useful attachment, but should be of the sort which uses a hook stud on the near side, so that it can be fixed or removed without having to take the cavesson over the horse's ears. A nose strap can also be attached from the noseband to headpiece if required, in order to prevent the noseband from sagging.

The Wels cavesson is less complex in design, and is really just a strong noseband with the three rings attached, and a jowl strap.

TACK TIP

When buying a cavesson select one that has two rings or 'Ds' just behind the cheekpieces on the noseband to which a bit can be attached. This is of great help when first bitting the young horse, as a bit can easily be introduced by strapping it in place on the cavesson, rather than having to fit a bridle as well.

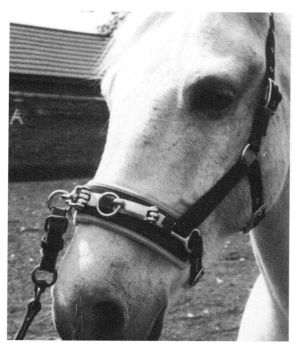

A correctly fitted webbing lungeing cavesson.

Lungeing Rein with Swivel Hook

Lungeing reins (or lunge lines) are usually made of tubular web, cord or cotton. Cheap nylon ones can be bought, but they are often found to be slippery and too light to maintain an even contact with the horse's nose. In length they range from between 6 and 10m (6½ and 11yds). They are usually fixed to the cavesson by means of a strap and buckle or a snap hook; however, a swivel attachment should join the body of the lunge rein to the fixing device to facilitate free movement at all times. The end of the lunge rein ends in a loop for holding on to. It is always wise to wear gloves when lungeing to prevent a nasty burn if the rein is pulled sharply through your hands.

Most people use two lunge reins for long-reining work; it is possible to buy leather long reins made for the purpose, although these are expensive.

Lungeing Roller

Lungeing rollers have two main purposes. They act as a pre-saddling device in order to accustom the horse to weight on his back, and as an anchorage point to which side reins or other schooling devices can be attached if required. They are made of either leather or web and the best designs have adjustment straps on both sides (so, in effect, the roller comes in two halves comprising the top section and a belly band). Down both sides of the roller there should be a series of rings (at least three) which allows reins to be attached at various heights as the trainer wishes. Any breaking roller should have padded panels on either side of the horse's wither to prevent rubbing and thus a sore back. In between these two panels on the topside of the roller there should be a further two rings, one to the front on which to attach various schooling aids, if required, and one to the rear to which a crupper can be fitted (*see* Chapter 6). The belly band should be cut back at the elbow akin to an Atherstone girth (*see* pages 97–98) to prevent pinching and rubbing. When fitting the roller, make certain it sits securely in the horse's sternum curve: this will ensure that the roller does not interfere with the horse's shoulder movement.

A breaking roller should be fitted with a detachable breastgirth. This will help to keep it in place on horses in round, soft condition. As they become fitter, the belly band will sit well in to the sternum curve and so the breastgirth can be dispensed with.

Wither Pad

A wither pad is necessary for added protection where either the roller has no padded wither panels, or the horse has a high wither. It can be a simple folded-up stable rubber, a piece of foam or a gel pad. These gel pads are a fairly recent innovation and they are excellent. They stay put in the most awkward of places and thus relieve much discomfort.

Lungeing Whip

A lungeing whip is essential when lungeing. Although it is used as a driving aid rather than as a punishment, it needs to be long enough to touch the horse when he is on full lunge. While this rarely happens, it may be necessary just to touch (not hit) the horse with the whip on occasion, for it becomes ineffective if he knows it cannot reach him. Consideration also needs to be given to the weight and balance of the whip to match your hand size and strength. Correctly balanced for you, and its action will be instant and precise; too light or too heavy and its action will be clumsy and delayed. The modern nylon or fibreglass whips are suitably flexible and well balanced.

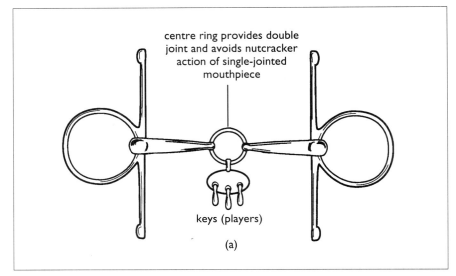

centre ring provides double joint and avoids nutcracker action of single-jointed mouthpiece

keys (players)

(a)

Mouthing bits:
(a) double-jointed cheek snaffle;

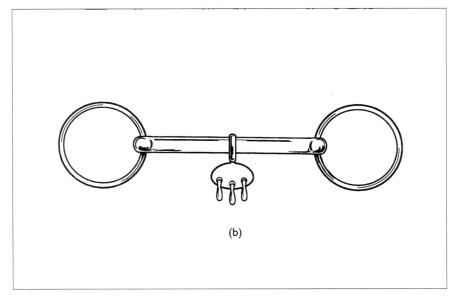

(b)

(b) loose-ring straight bar.

A Chifney anti-rearing bit.

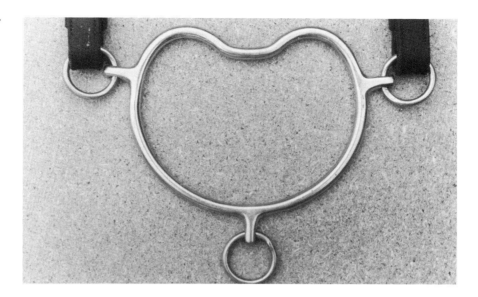

Mouthing Bits

These are straight-bar or jointed snaffles with 'keys' in the centre, which are introduced before and while lungeing the horse in preparation for riding. The purpose of the keys is to help the horse play and mouth with the bit, encouraging him to salivate and thus relax the jaw and accept the bit. The most common mouthing bits with keys are the double-jointed cheek snaffle, the loose-ring straight-bar snaffle and the loose-ring wooden straight-bar snaffle. However, their value is questionable and a more sensible approach is to start as you mean to go on, and introduce the horse to a simple snaffle from the outset. This may be a straight bar initially to 'mouth' the horse, moving on to a jointed one as soon as the wearing of a bit has been accepted. Young horses benefit from having cheeks on their bits, as this prevents them from being pulled through the mouth in early training and offers a guiding action. A Fulmer snaffle is a good bit to start with for early training.

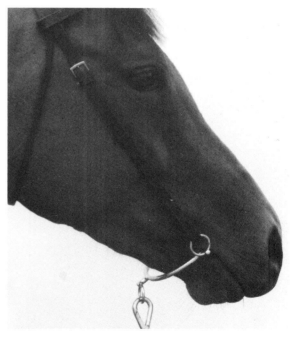

The Chifney correctly fitted.

Chifney (Anti-Rearing) Bit

A Chifney bit is often used on youngsters or stallions when in-hand, but only as a restraint, not as an acceptable everyday bit. Once the horse has learnt how to behave correctly and you have him in control, this type of bit should be dispensed with.

121

9 Boots and Bandages

Protecting your horse's legs requires a great deal of consideration; a reality borne out by the fact that developments in bandages and boots are more widely researched than in any other area of horse equipment. New materials with high-impact absorption are being developed and incorporated into boots (and some bandaging materials) all the time, but the busy horseowner has some very basic needs which must not be overlooked:

- Ease of application;
- Speed of application;
- Security once in place;
- Protection and support offered.

When jumping, the practice of bandaging the horse's legs used to be considered essential, but nowadays it is more usual to see horses wearing protective boots. Boots are also suitable for everyday exercise and schooling. In fact, it would be more unusual to see a horse being ridden without boots than with them.

BOOTS

Types of Boot

Brushing Boots
These are worn by the majority of horses for all kinds of ridden work. Their purpose is to provide a barrier between the fetlock joints, as many horses rub these together when being ridden, which is known as brushing. Instead, the two boots will rub together which prevents bruising and grazes. They should always be

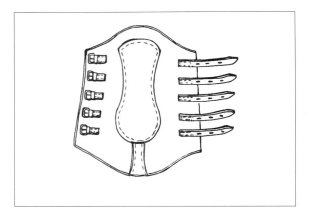

Speedicut boot.

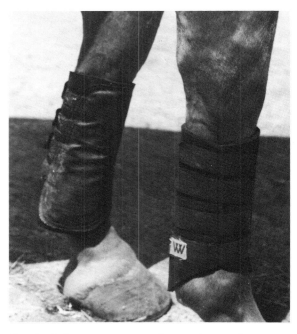

Synthetic boots are extremely popular as they are easy to keep clean and, with velcro fastenings, easy to fit.

used on young horses when being schooled or lunged as often they cannot get their footsteps in order, and so brush until their movement becomes more rhythmical.

They can be made of leather with a felt lining, although these are being superseded by synthetic materials as they are easier to fit (having velcro fastenings), easier to keep clean and do not absorb water. In order to offer maximum protection most have a hardened shield on the inside of the leg. They should be fitted so that they come to just below the fetlock joint on the inside of the leg and just above it on the outside. They extend up to a few inches from the knee or hock.

Speedicut Boots

Where a horse brushes badly, he may injure himself higher up than normal, which is known as speedicutting. In this case, a variation of the normal brushing boot is used, called a speedicut boot. This is the same as a brushing boot on the lower half, but extends up the inside of the leg until it reaches just under the knee or hock.

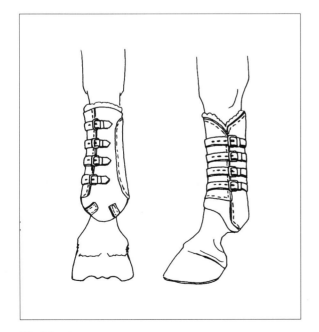

Heel boots.

Fetlock Boots

These are another variation of the brushing boot and are used for the same purpose. However, they are shorter than the normal brushing boots and may only cover the joint, hence they are also known as ankle boots.

Heel Boots

These are used during particularly fast work or when undertaking demanding jumping. They fit tightly around the lower leg, from just below the knee or hock, down to and around the back of the fetlock joint. When fitted to the forelegs they will protect a horse from striking into himself with his hind shoes, but will also prevent injuries to the fetlocks and ergots, should they come into contact with the ground as they can when at maximum stretch.

Polo Boots

These are very robust boots, designed to offer maximum protection during the sometimes rough sport of polo. They start as a heavy-duty brushing boot, but extend down over the pastern and coronet, thus protecting the whole of the lower leg. It is crucial that they are fastened correctly, as a loose boot can bring a horse down from great speeds, causing severe injury. They may be fastened with straps and buckles, with an additional strap fastening around the pastern to prevent them from flapping, or they can be bandaged in place. More often than not they are both strapped on and bandaged for a fail-safe system.

Tendon Boots

These are designed to offer support to the tendon while the horse is doing strenuous work, and also offer protection from a horse striking into himself, known as a high overreach. They can be open fronted or completely closed in depending on whether protection over fences is also required or not. They usually have a protective shield running down the rear of the boot, which is often padded. They may be made of leather or synthetic materials.

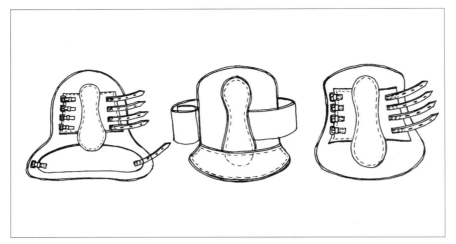

Various types of polo boot.

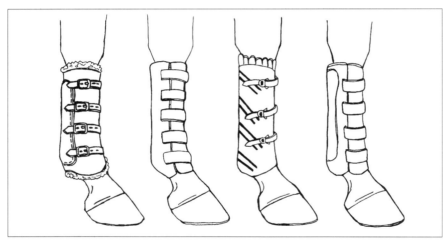

Various types of tendon boot.

Shin Boots

These are the reverse of a tendon boot in that the protective shield runs down the front of the leg, to offer protection to the shin from knocks when jumping. However, the two types of boot are shaped differently and so they are not interchangeable.

Yorkshire Boots

They are simply a rectangular piece of felt, or similar material with a tape sewn right through the middle. This is then placed on the leg, so the tape is secured just above the fetlock joint. The upper half of the pad is then folded down, providing a double thickness of felt over the joint. They are deemed more suitable for horses which only brush lightly, as they have no weight and do not interfere with natural movement.

Anti-brushing Rings

These are narrow rubber rings, which attach around the fetlock joint by means of a strap and buckle. Only one is used, on the leg most prone to injury. The idea is that the opposing leg will be prevented from rubbing against the injured leg, thus allowing any injury to heal and preventing further ones. In practice, they do interfere with a horse's action and can make them stumble.

124

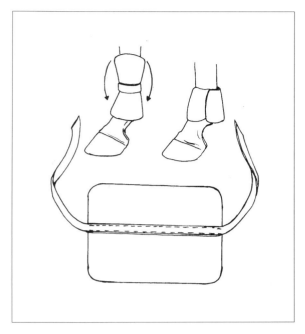

Yorkshire boots and how they fit.

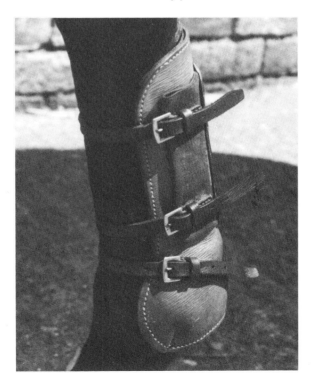

An open-fronted tendon boot.

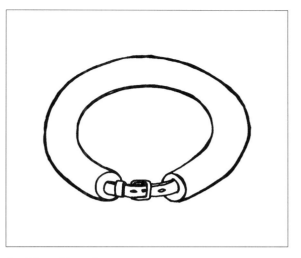

Anti-brushing ring.

Overreach Boots

These are often called 'bell boots' due to their shape. They fit over the hoof to protect the bulbs of the heel on the foreleg from being struck into by the hind shoe during fast work or jumping. They are made of rubber, and either just simply pull over the hoof or are fastened by means of buckles, strap and slots or velcro fastenings. When buying a pair, make sure they are not so long that they drag on the ground as this can be extremely annoying for the horse, and may cause the boots to flip up. Petal overreach boots are a variation that aim to overcome the problem of overreach boots flipping up during use. Instead of the continuous band, they have individual sections running all the way around the hoof, which overlap each other. They make a peculiar noise when the horse is moving at speed, but are nonetheless very effective.

Skeleton Knee Pads

These are lightweight knee boots designed for use when riding on the roads to prevent broken knees in the event of a fall. They are simply a hard leather knee shield which is secured by a padded band strapped above the knee. They have no lower strap so do not interfere with movement.

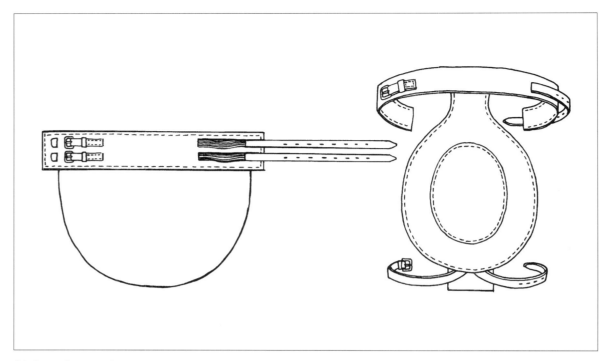

Skeleton knee pads.

Fitting Boots

- Boots come in pairs and a front pair is always shorter than a hind pair, and usually have one less strap.
- Always ensure the straps are on the outside of the leg and face backwards, except knee and hock boots which face forwards.
- To prevent the boot from sliding down the leg if the horse moves, always do up the middle strap first to secure the boot.
- Always use any keeper provided.
- Always keep velcro fittings free from fluff and dirt as they become far less effective when dirty.
- Fasten boots tight enough so that they will not slip, but not so tight that they will interfere with circulation. As with bandages, the pressure should be even all the way down and around the leg.
- When taking boots off, always work from the bottom upwards.

The simple pull-on type of overreach boot.

BANDAGES

Traditionally, where support bandages are applied for exercise, or on jumping horses, they have a layer of padding underneath (either gauze and cotton, foam-filled pads or porter boots). However, there are now alternatives in the form of cushioned support bandages which do not require padding underneath, but still provide protection from knocks, abrasions or strain.

Apply an exercise or support bandage as follows (*see* illustration below):

1. Make sure your horse's legs are thoroughly clean and dry. If using cushioned bandages go to step 4.
2. If using padding, cut a piece to the correct size so that it will cover from under the knee to just below the fetlock.
3. Wrap the padding around the leg so that it is firm and the open end lies on the outside of the leg, facing backwards.
4. Unroll the bandage by 5–7cm (2–3in), then hold it on to the leg just below the knee so that the loose end is free. Start to wind the bandage around the leg in the same direction as the padding (if used) until you have completed one whole turn. Then flap the free end down so that it will be covered the next time the bandage is coiled around the leg. This prevents the bandage from working loose and coming undone at the top.
5. Carry on down the leg covering just over half of the width of the bandage on each turn as you go. It is important to achieve an even pressure all the way down the leg – not so tight that it will restrict the horse's circulation and not so loose that the bandage will slip off. To do this, stretch the bandage to its full potential and then let it come back to half stretch before applying.
6. When you reach the point just above the fetlock joint, start to work your way up again maintaining the same pressure. (Some modern bandages are applied around and to just below the fetlock joint, but this needs to be done with caution if it is not to affect the movement of the joint. It is more usual to see this type of technique applied when bandaging an injury – *see* the end of this chapter.) About an inch of padding should be seen below the last turn of the bandage.

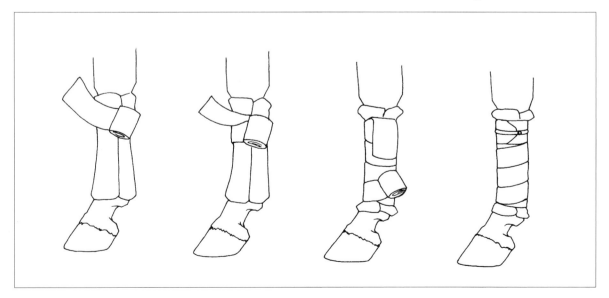

Correct procedure for applying exercise bandages.

127

7. Work back up the leg as before. The aim is to finish about an inch from the top of the bandage. Take the tapes around the leg once (or twice if they are exceptionally long) ensuring you secure them with a bow on the *outside* of the leg, still maintaining an even pressure. If you do the tapes up on the inside of the leg, the horse could rub them loose.

8. There are various ways of preventing the tapes from hanging loose, which could leave them open to be pulled or rubbed undone. If the bandage is only to cover a dressing then you can simply fold the turn of the bandage above the tapes, down over them. If you are going to do any fast work or jumping it is sensible to protect them securely, either by using two full wraps of highly sticky tape or by sewing them.

Leg Protector Pads

Prolite is well known as a gel pad for use under saddles, but by varying the mix of gel to latex, a high-impact absorption Prolite has been created, which is ideal as leg protector pads under bandages. The protector pads are extremely lightweight and are effective in preventing injuries caused by a horse striking into itself or hitting a fence across country. They also conform well to the contours of the horse's leg which, coupled with the absorption factor, helps to prevent overtightening of bandages.

Porter boots are also ideal to be bandaged over. They are made of expanded plastizole, a lightweight close cell solid foam that is moulded to the horse's leg. They do not absorb water so the leg protection does not become wet and heavy on the cross-country course and they will neither stretch nor shrink in use.

Bandaging for Stable or Travelling

Stable or travelling bandages extend from just under the knee to the coronet. They always have padding underneath, so the piece used needs to be long enough to cover this distance.

You can now get special foam-filled padding which has rounded knee pads incorporated and these are excellent for added protection. Stable bandages are usually made of woollen material or stockinet and are used as protection when travelling, as protection over injuries, or to keep 'filled legs' down where horses are standing in their stables for long periods.

1. Start the bandage in the same manner as the exercise bandage. Once you get to the fetlock joint carry on down to the coronet in a criss-cross fashion so that you have an inverted V at the centre of the coronet, then work your way back up the leg and finish off, as with an exercise bandage.

2. Many stable bandages have velcro fastenings. These are safe as long as the velcro is cleared of any bits of fluff or straw. If the velcro becomes clogged, it becomes less effective and the bandage could come undone.

3. If you bandage one leg because of any injury, always bandage the opposite leg as well. The horse will compensate for the bad leg by putting all his weight on to the good one, so a bandage will offer some support.

Tail Bandaging

When bandaging a tail, no padding is needed. Start at the very top, ensuring that all loose hairs are tucked in. Work down the tail, as when bandaging a leg, until you nearly reach the end of the dock, then work back up again. Fasten as normal. To remove a tail bandage, do not unravel it all. Simply undo the tapes and slide it off downwards. This will make the tail lie flat, creating a good appearance.

TACK TIP

Water absorption in boots and bandages is a point often overlooked. Having jumped into or gone through water, materials such as felt which soak up water like a sponge, result in your horse having to carry an extra pound of weight on each leg for the rest of the course.

128

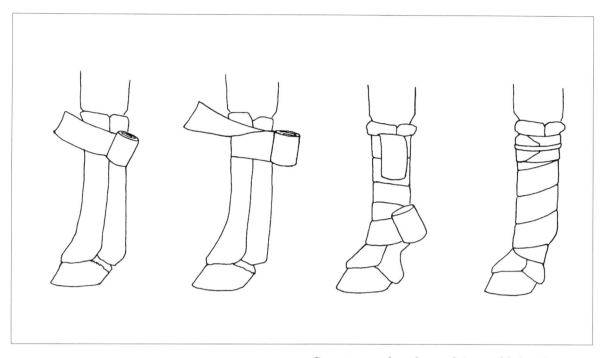

Correct procedure for applying stable bandages.

When bandaging due to injury, always bandage both legs, as a horse will compensate for his hurting leg by putting all his weight on the good one.

Travelling Boots

Nowadays travelling boots are all-in-one designs, protecting from the coronet right up to and over the knees and hocks. They come in various materials which are light and well padded. They are easily cleaned and comfortable for the horse to wear so, all in all, preparing horses for travelling is a relatively quick and simple task.

Where a horse is bandaged for travelling you will need to fit additional protective items, which may include some or all of the following depending on your type of horsebox or trailer and the way your horse travels.

Coronet Boots

These are like an overreach boot, but are made of felt or leather. They fit over the coronet and hoof to protect them from injuries during travelling. However, overreach boots can be worn instead, on all four feet and, if anything, offer better protection.

Knee Boots and Hock Boots

These are used where shorter travelling boots or bandages are fitted. They have blocked and padded joint shields which are surrounded by a felt or woollen material to provide good protection from knocks during the journey. Each boot has two straps. One lies over a padded cuff above the joint and does up securely but not so tightly that it would interfere with circulation (many have an elastic insert to combat overtightening). The other strap does up loosely below the knee as its only purpose is to prevent the whole thing from flapping about.

Poll Guards

These are made of padded foam, felt, leather, leather-covered fibreglass or synthetic materials and are designed to prevent the horse from hitting his poll on the roof of the lorry when loading and travelling. They attach to the headcollar, which prevents them from slipping down over the face and scaring the horse.

TAIL GUARDS

Have you ever arrived at a show and, upon unloading your horse, found that he has a very ruffled and rubbed dock, and an extremely mucky tail where he has been sitting on the side of the lorry or trailer ramp? Most of us have and it can be infuriating, especially if you are pushed for time and due to go in the ring at any minute. When using an ordinary tail bandage or tailguard, or both, does not work, the Enduro Tail Traveller could provide the answer. During trials, this simple idea proved totally effective at getting the horse to the show, still in 'show condition' and ready to compete. It is a tailguard made of polypropylene (a rot-proof material), with a pocket at the bottom into which the lower half of the horse's tail is put, thus totally enclosing the tail to prevent it from being rubbed or becoming soiled or tangled. It can be secured in three

Nowadays travelling boots are all-in-one designs.

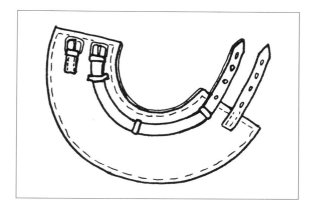

Coronet boot.

Travelling hock boot.

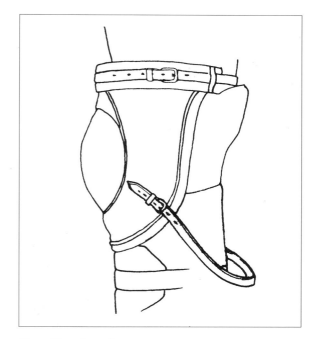

Travelling knee boot.

ways: either by fixing to the D-ring on some rugs; attachment to tabs supplied with it that you simply sew on to your travelling rug; or attachment to a neck/roller strap for use with or without a rug. There is no need to use a tail bandage underneath, although it will accommodate one should you wish to use it to lay a pulled tail.

EQUIPMENT FOR INJURY

Most horses will at some time or another either sustain some sort of injury to the leg, or suffer from leg strain. In order to relieve pain, and to prevent further damage or strain, the leg should be protected with boots and/or bandages as appropriate.

Types of Boot

Hose Boots
These are like an exercise boot to which a hose can be attached. They save you from having to stand holding a cold hose on your horse's leg for half and hour, as you can simply fit the boot, turn on the hose and get on with grooming or some other chore while supervising your horse.

Cooling Packs
There are many types of cooling pack, but they all have the same objective: to cool the leg and reduce swelling and thus offer pain relief.

131

Correctly prepared for travelling.

They are frozen until needed, when they are simply bandaged on to the injured leg to cool it. Make sure that their outer covering will prevent ice burns. If you are unsure about this, bandage them on over the top of protective padding.

Equiboots or Easyboots

The equiboot has been around for quite some time now, and a newer improved design is the easyboot. They are ideally suited to keeping dressings in place, or for securing poultices on to the foot. The dressing or poultice is put on in the normal way and the horse's foot is slipped into the boot. It is then tightened up and the horse can walk about without getting the dressing dirty or wet, with the additional benefit that the horse can be turned out as usual. They are also ideal for the horse prone to getting punctured soles while turned out in the field. They have also been used to keep a horse in work when for some reason he cannot be shod.

Poultice Boot

This is another veterinary boot designed to keep dressings or poultices in place. However, it is really like a 'boot' in that the horse slips

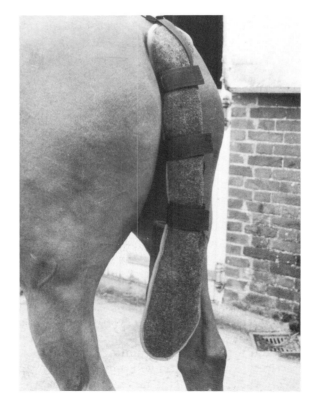

The innovative Enduro Tail Traveller which gets the horse to the show with a spanking clean and unrubbed tail.

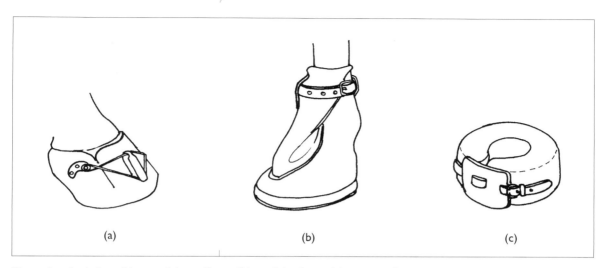

Boots for the injured horse: (a) equiboot; (b) poultice boot; (c) sausage boot.

his whole leg into it, like wearing a wellington. They are ideal where the horse has injuries to his fetlock joints and coronet, rather than just his hooves.

Sausage Boots

These are used to prevent the horse from bruising his elbow with his shoe while lying in the stable or field, thus preventing capped elbows. They are thick padded rings of leather which look like a doughnut and are fitted around the fetlock as needed.

Bonner Bandages

The Bonner bandage offers a combination of cold and compression therapy in the treatment of swelling, inflammation and painful conditions of the muscles, tendons and ligaments. It is specifically designed to be soaked in water and then frozen, yet it remains flexible enough to mould easily to the leg or joint. It freezes within ten minutes and is then applied to the affected area for fifteen minutes, whereupon after removal, the area will remain cold for up to one hour. It contains no medication, is safe for repeated applications and can be used as a preventative aid for competition horses after a strenuous day. The Bonner bandage should be an essential part of your first-aid kit for leg swelling, strains, sprains or bruising

Bandaging Injuries

Traditionally, when bandaging injuries it is common to use cohesive support bandages over dressings and poultices. However, unless you are experienced in using such bandages it is difficult to maintain a consistent pressure throughout. Flexus is a new type of cohesive adherent support bandage used to provide cushioned support and compression without the risk of pressure increase after application. They really do hold dressings firmly in place, but with a lower pressure than other elasticized bandages, making them very easy to apply at the correct tension.

They are water repellent and breathable, do not loosen over time and will not slip once applied. For competition horses the elastic fabric and cohesive system provides a consistent level of support throughout all gaits, moving with limb expansion and contraction but without the build-up of pressure points.

10 Shoes and Studs ──────

Shoes are an integral part of the riding or driving horse's equipment, although they are not an item that you tend to give much consideration to. This is because you have little to do with the selection or fitting of them, as this is the farrier's job. However, it is worth learning something about them, if for no other reason than that it will help you to understand why the farrier may advise the fitting of a particular shoe, and give you a better insight into what can go wrong and why. Studs, on the other hand, can be fitted by you, although the farrier will have to make a shoe to accept them.

SHOES

Shoes are made of wrought iron, aluminium and steel and can be mass produced or hand made. There are many different types of shoe in use for a variety of reasons. However, shoes are mainly used to protect the hooves from wear and damage. In some cases, special shoes are made up to correct faulty action, or to offer support for an abnormality or injury; this is known as remedial shoeing.

Types of Shoe

Fullered Shoes
The most common shoe and the one fitted to the majority of horses is the fullered shoe. This is a fairly lightweight shoe (weighing between 400 and 525g/14.5 and 18.5oz), used to protect the horse's hooves while undertaking ridden or driven work on hard surfaces. It has a nail channel running through its centre which permits the nails to sit almost flush with the surface of the shoe, and because it collects dirt and grit, also offers a non-slip surface. If the nails were not sunk in they would quickly wear away and the shoe would fall off. The surface which butts up to the sole of the hoof is wider than the floor bearing one.

As with most shoes, the fullered shoe has three nail holes on the inside of the hoof and four on the outside. The front shoes have one toe clip in the centre, while the hind shoes can either be rolled, or have two toe clips, one on either side of the hoof, to prevent the shoe from moving. The front shoes are often rounded off at the heel to prevent the hind shoe from catching on them and ripping them off. This is known as pencilling.

Stamped Shoes
These are fairly coarse shoes used on heavy horses, or large driving horses. They consist of a single hoof-shaped bar of iron, which simply has nail holes stamped in.

Feather-edged Shoes
These are also known as anti-brushing shoes as they are designed to prevent the horse from damaging himself when he brushes. The inner branch of the fore or hind shoes is narrower than the outer branch.

Grass Tips
These are half shoes which only cover the toe and quarter of the hoof. They are designed to be worn by horses at grass whose hooves are in poor condition. They may also be used in remedial shoeing to raise the toe and thus lower the heel.

Three-quarter Shoes

These shoes have the inside of the heel removed so that they only provide support for the toe and the outside of the hoof. They are used to relieve pressure from an injured site, or alternatively where the horse has a corn. They are designed in the same way as a fullered shoe.

Bar Shoes

There are various types of bar shoe. Some have the heels folded back over the frog and joined while others have a cross bar running vertically across the hoof. There are a variety of reasons for their employment; for example they may offer relief to a horse suffering from navicular or laminitis, or they may be used to

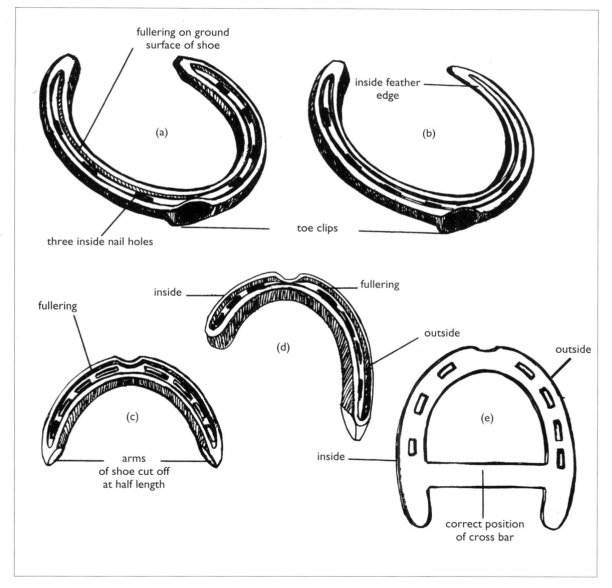

Types of shoe: (a) fullered; (b) feather-edged; (c) grass tip; (d) three-quarter shoe; (e) bar shoe.

help the frog function properly, limiting sole contact with the ground.

Racing Plates
These are lightweight aluminium or alloy shoes, used on racehorses for the duration of the race only. They are very short wearing, so normal riding shoes should be fitted for everyday exercise.

TACK TIP
If your horse does a lot of road work ask your farrier about fitting frost nails. These have tungsten tips which offer more grip and are much harder wearing, so your horse's shoes will last longer. They also provide added security on frosty mornings – hence their name!

ALTERNATIVES

Where nail-on shoes do not prove to be ideal, a good alternative is an **easyboot**. These are quite similar in concept to human shoes, in that the hoof slips inside and is secured in place. They are made from lightweight polyurethane, which prevents bruising of the soles, and last three times as long as a steel shoe during constant use. For regular use they are popular among endurance riders as they do not result in nail holes which weaken hooves. They also provide greater traction than steel shoes, and their cushioned insoles reduce jarring.

With traditional shoes, you have to have your horse shod every six weeks or so, even if you ride only occasionally. Easyboots are therefore economical for weekend or occasional riders; just have the horse trimmed up as necessary in between times.

We all know how infuriating it can be if a horse loses a shoe just before or during a competition. An easyboot can provide a 'spare type' in such cases until the blacksmith can attend. It is also ideal for keeping a poultice in place, or the hoof dry and clean during treatment (*see* page 132).

Plastic shoes are another alternative where there is a problem with normal shoeing. They are bonded to the horse's hoof by means of glue and are a good solution where nail holes have caused the wall to split. They will wear well for about four weeks of average exercise.

PROTECTIVE PADS

Where a horse's sole or frog is susceptible to bruising it is often useful to fit leather pads under the shoes. These will also help to reduce the effects of concussion. Where it is desirable to reduce the angle of the foot with the ground, perhaps where a horse has long sloping pasterns, a wedged plastic pad can be fitted under the shoe. These are quite tough and because they have an absorbency factor, also offer greater protection for the soles than leather pads.

STUDS

There are two main reasons why your horse may need to be fitted with studs: either to prevent him from slipping on the roads, or to help him get a grip in less than ideal conditions during competitions. Whatever anyone might tell you, studs are not good for your horse's fetlock joints; however, they are a necessary evil because without them you risk falling over in hard or slippy conditions, which could be far worse.

There is a great variety of shapes and sizes to choose from, although most have a tungsten core for durability. Choosing the correct type will depend on the ground, the type of shoes in use and the activity in which your horse is participating. Generally, the harder the ground the more pointed the stud and the softer the ground the squarer the stud; but remember: perfect ground means no studs should be required. In reality, however, we hardly ever get perfect ground and, in any case, good going underfoot may be spoiled by

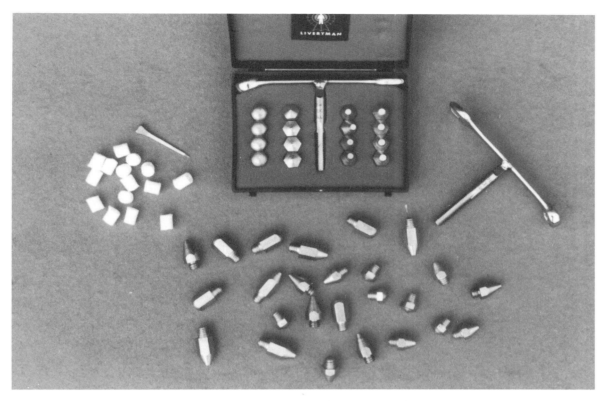

Keep all your studs, taps and hole protectors together so they are ready for use whenever needed.

wet, slippy grass; so, as many top riders will tell you, studs can make the difference between winning or losing a competition.

Many people put only one stud on the outside of each shoe, but this drags one-sidedly on the horse's joints. While the stud sinks into the ground this pull is minimal, but what happens when the stud hits harder ground? Obviously the outside of the horse's hoof is tipped upwards, which affects the joints in the leg. Horses' fetlock joints have no lateral movement so such an occurrence will unbalance and stress the leg. You might not notice any effects immediately as they will be minimal each time. But as these occurrences of stress stack up, come two of three years down the line your horse may go lame as his leg finally 'gives up'.

To minimize any damage it is preferable to use two studs on each foot, one either side, so a horse completely studded up will be wearing eight studs. If the ground is hard you might use small pointed studs on the front feet and medium pointed ones on the hind. If the ground is soft you might use small square studs in front and large square ones behind (remember, it is your horse's hindlegs which are more likely to lose their footing). Furthermore, always ensure that you do not put studs into shoes which have worn thin. If you do, it will result in the end of the stud driving into the sole of the hoof!

TACK TIP

When using pointed studs in the front feet, horses that snatch their front legs up tightly over a fence can stud themselves behind the girth, so it may be necessary to use a stud guard or 'belly pad' which attaches to the girth.

137

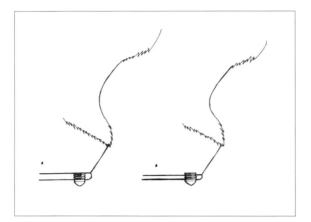

Always make sure that shoes are not worn thin when using studs.

Types of Stud

There are many different studs, although most activities will see the use of one of the following six:

Road Studs
These are for hacking out on the roads to provide grip and durability for the shoes.

Standard Jump Studs
These are fairly small, tapered studs to provide extra grip in good going, but where the conditions (perhaps dewy or rainy) might prove slippery.

Pointed Jump Studs
These are for use in firm ground as they will penetrate the soil, offering hold without jarring the legs. They are ideal for all disciplines in such conditions, including dressage and showing.

Large Jump Studs
These are longer than other studs and the end tapers off so that it will enter the ground more easily if it is slightly firm. They are usually used on the hind feet of horses undertaking demanding showjumping or cross-country courses.

A stud guard will protect the horse from puncturing his skin with the studs should he snatch his feet up tightly.

Dome Top Stud
These are another long stud but do not taper at the end. Instead the end is dome shaped. They, too, are designed for demanding jumping, especially where maximum grip is required in soft going.

Sharp Stud
These have a round tapered barrel coming out of a square base. They are designed to penetrate hard ground, with the square base providing plenty of hold. They are used in all disciplines.

Fitting Studs

1.   The first step in the use of studs is having your farrier put stud holes into your horse's

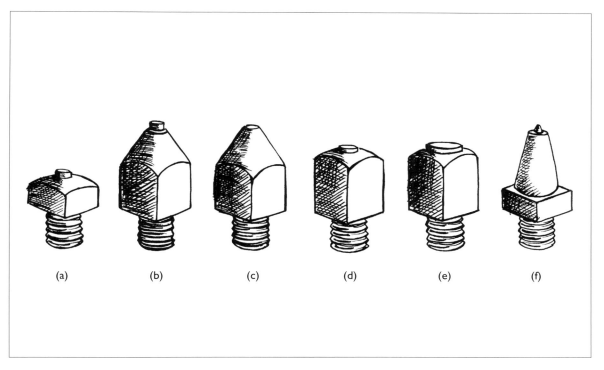

Types of stud: (a) road stud; (b) standard jump stud; (c) pointed jump stud; (d) large jump stud; (e) dome top stud; (f) sharp stud.

shoes. These should then be plugged as described on this page.

2. Before putting in any stud you will need to remove this plug, so keep a horseshoe nail handy for doing so.

3. Place the stud tap into the holes and screw down to clean the thread. Do not allow your horse to put his foot down while using the tap and be careful to keep the tap square, or else you will damage the thread.

4. While still holding the hoof up, select an appropriate stud and screw it into the hole. Use the other end of the tap to make sure it is tight.

5. Make sure you use the same type of studs on both front shoes, or back shoes.

Protection of Stud Holes

In order to prevent the stud holes from becoming clogged with mud and becoming rusty, it is essential to pack them out immediately the stud is removed. You can do this by making a plug of cotton wool smeared in Vaseline, or you can buy purpose made stud 'sleepers' to plug the holes. Make sure you push any plug right in and that it plugs the hole out right to the top – a horseshoe nail is ideal for the job.

TACK TIP

Having finished in competition, remember to remove the studs before putting your horse on to the lorry or walking him on to a hard surface. Leaving them in while travelling home is like expecting a man to take standing room on a train in stiletto shoes.

TACK TIP

When studs are not in use, keep them wrapped in an oily rag and put them into a polythene box together with the stud tap, plugs and spare horseshoe nail so that they are all to hand when you need them.

---

11 Rugs and Horse Clothing

Buying a new rug (or rugs, as is usually the case) is an expensive business, so you must choose carefully. However, rugs come in a bewildering number of styles, fabrics and colours nowadays, so selecting the most appropriate one might prove to be very difficult. The main points to remember when selecting a rug are that the length, depth and shape are correct for your horse. Then it is just a case of making sure you fit it correctly and look after it properly. A quality rug is usually a good investment, provided it is well cared for.

FITTING

Irrespective of type, a correct fit is all important if the rug is to stay in place and be comfortable. Rugs are usually sized in 7.5cm (3in) increments starting at about 99cm (3ft 6in) up to about 198cm (6ft 6in). However, it is not very helpful to make any generalisations about what size of rug will fit what height of horse, as a broad horse may need a bigger rug than a thinner one of the same height, or perhaps a different make or style which might be a more generous fit.

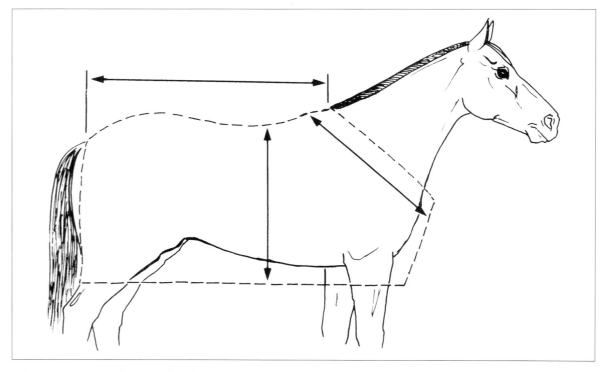

Measurements to take when buying a new rug.

Correct fit is all important if a rug is to be comfortable and stay in place.

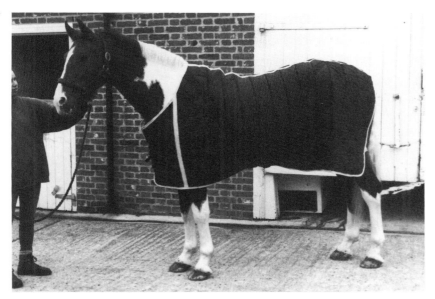

Having got the right size, it is important that you put it on and fasten it correctly. While the older horse might tolerate you throwing a rug straight over his back, a younger or more nervous one will not appreciate it at all, so it is sensible always to practise a safe rugging technique:

1.   Before putting on a rug, firstly fold it in half by bringing the back up and over the front so that the inside lining is facing outwards. Gently lay this over the wither and saddle area of the back.
2.   Carefully fold the rug backwards over the quarters.
3.   Once in place, check that both sides are level so that one side does not hang lower than the other.
4.   Do up the chest straps, but do not pull the rug forward in order to do so as this will pull the hair the wrong way and make the horse uncomfortable. If you find the rug is too far back, take it off and replace it further up the neck, repeating steps 1–3.
5.   A lot of rugs have insufficient overlap at the chest. The front fastenings should allow the rug to close neatly together across the chest, without being taut. Many have a velcro strip at the chest which allows for a snug fit, with added security being provided by slip buckle fastenings which do up over the top. This allows for individual fitting, ensuring an optimum fit for each and every horse.
6.   Getting the tension right for the roller or cross-over surcingles is very important. They should be done up firmly enough to prevent the rug from shifting, but not as tightly as you would do up a girth. As a guide, you should easily be able to slip the flat of your hand between the straps and the horse's skin. A good rug with cross-over surcingles will have these so positioned that they do up in the centre of the horse's belly.
7.   Once everything is done up the rug should look 'right'. Stand back for an overall view.

The length of the rug will determine a good fit. Rugs are measured from the centre of the chest around the body to the rear of the quarters where the rug ends. The general impression of a rug once fitted should be a good overall fit, like a well-made, well-fitting coat for yourself. A rug will not stay in place unless it is correctly fitted, so it is essential to be sure

Getting the tension right for cross-over surcingles is important. They should admit the flat of the hand between strap and skin.

of your measurements before buying. Points to check for a good fit include:

The Withers
A well-fitting rug should lie just in front of the withers.

The Shoulders
To allow for free movement, the outside edge of the rug should be well in front of the shoulder. The front should not be too tight as it has to allow for the horse putting his head down to the floor. When the horse is standing still with his head tied up you should be able to get the width of two hands between your horse's chest and the straps.

The Rump
The rug should finish just as the tail starts. If the rug flops over the tail it will have a tendency to slip, whereas if the rug falls short of the tail the horse will become cold. The rug should also be a snug fit over the rump. This is achieved by correct shaping for your type of horse. One rug may fit your friend's 16.2hh. horse perfectly, while it puckers up over the rump of your own 16.2hh. horse.

TACK TIP
When trying on a new purchase, fit it over the top of a summer sheet so that in the event that it does not fit properly you can return it in a clean state.

STABLE RUGS

Warmth is very important when considering a suitable stable rug, as the horse will be forced to stand idle for much of the time and cannot trot about to keep warm as he might do in the field. Comfort is equally important as the horse will be wearing his stable rug for most of the day and night. Most modern stable rugs are made of padded or quilted material with a nylon outer and cotton lining, while traditional stable rugs were made of jute with a woollen liner. Many modern rugs are very lightweight but still able to keep the horse warm down to temperatures below freezing due to the use of specifically designed fibres which have unique reflective thermal properties. If you are not sure how warm a rug will be, ask the retailer for specific information.

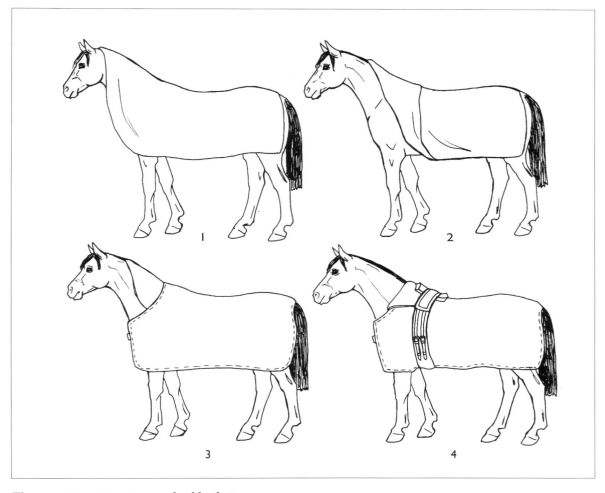

The correct way to put on under-blankets.

UNDER-BLANKETS

When the weather turns extremely cold, stable rugs can have further layers added underneath for extra warmth. These under-blankets need to be put on securely otherwise they will slip back as the horse moves or lies down.

1.   Fold the rug in half and, with the open end towards the horse's head, lay it over his neck. Fold it back until it comes to just in front of the base of the tail. The blanket should still be three-quarters of the way up the horse's neck.

2.   Fold each front corner up to the withers to form a point on the neck.

3.   Put on the stable rug and secure as normal.

4.   Fold the point back along the withers securing it with a roller and pad. Make sure that the point is flat and not crumpled up as this will put pressure on the withers and make the horse's back sore.

Alternatives for under-blankets include another, more lightweight stable rug, a cooler, a summer sheet, or a specially made clip-in lining which is designed to go with certain types of rug.

143

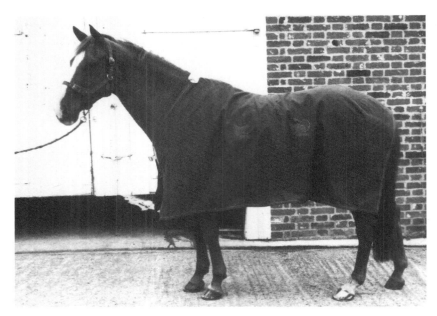

Most New Zealand rugs are made of waxed cotton or canvas. This one is extra deep so that it will right itself after being rolled in.

NEW ZEALAND AND TURNOUT RUGS

These are designed for use while the horse is turned out in the paddock, to keep him warm and protect him from inclement weather. 'New Zealand' is a general term for rugs suitable for a horse to wear when permanently turned out, while 'turnout' can mean that a rug is suitable for permanent wear, or is only intended for a stabled horse who is turned out for short periods (such a rug is correctly known as a paddock rug), so check specific usage before you buy. Most New Zealand rugs are now made of waxed cotton or canvas, while turnout rugs are mostly made of synthetic materials. The depth of New Zealand rugs is all important, for protection as well as preventing them from slipping. The sides of the rug should be long enough so that none of the horse's belly is visible. This will ensure that the rug is self-righting after rolling and will protect the horse in all weathers.

All traditional New Zealand rugs have hind leg straps, and some also have front leg straps as well; while some modern turnout rugs do not have any but are shaped over the quarters and come with a tough fillet string to keep them in place. As long as the rug is deep enough, this seems to work well, especially for horses who object to rear leg straps or have sores due to previously poorly adjusted ones. With a turnout, or New Zealand rug, you need to fit the hind straps so that they are not so tight that they rub when the horse moves, or so loose that the horse can get his hooves through them when he lies down. Link one strap through the other and adjust them both until they allow the width of your hand between them and the horse's legs. Having done them up, ask someone to walk your horse on and view the straps from the rear – do they allow free movement?

Some other terms which you will find in literature about outdoor rugs are:

Ripstop
This indicates that the rug is made of a tough man-made fabric which will prevent many of the small tears made by branches and the like. However, it is not a guarantee that the rug will not rip – barbed wire will rip anything!

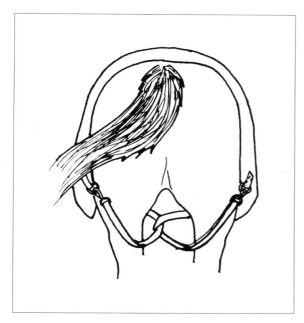

The hind leg straps on a New Zealand rug link through each other.

Extra Deep
This simply means that the rug is longer on each side of the horse than an ordinary rug.

Self-righting
Such a rug will fall back into place after rolling or excessive movement. It has leg straps, rather than cross-over surcingles, which are responsible for pulling the rug back into place.

Breathable
This type of rug has a water-resistant membrane under its outer fabric which permits vapour to pass through the fabric and then evaporate moisture. However, it will prove difficult to have a breathable rug which also has a highly water-resistant outer fabric.

DAY RUGS

In days gone by the horse would have had his jute night rug changed for a lighter day rug.

This practice has largely been dispensed with as modern fabrics are both lightweight and breathable, so one rug does for night and day.

SWEAT RUGS AND COOLERS

These look like a large string vest and are designed to cool the horse off and prevent him from getting a chill after work. The important thing to bear in mind when drying a horse off in this way is that a sweat rug alone is not sufficient. It is designed to cool the horse by encouraging the evaporation of moisture, but unless the weather is particularly hot, the horse is also liable to get a chill. To prevent this, you need to form an insulating layer of warm air by placing another lightweight sheet over the top. The front can be folded back to encourage air flow, and the whole secured with a roller. However, always ensure that where a roller is used, it has padding underneath and that the rug is not wrinkled up at the girth.

Coolers also fulfil a similar role, but with only one rug. Most modern coolers are specially designed to take moisture away from the horse and are therefore ideal as a winter cooler as they can be put on the horse while he is still damp. They also double as stable/travelling rugs, so are a good money saver, too!

EXERCISE SHEET

These are used to prevent clipped horses from getting cold while being exercised in cold weather. This prevents their muscles from getting cold and becoming liable to cramp. They may be made of wool or of waterproof fabric or even fluorescent material, which is ideal when riding on the roads in dull winter conditions.

They are put on forward of the withers, the saddle is put on over the top and the front corners are tucked well up under the girth straps. This allows for air circulation but also

To prevent a wet horse from catching a chill an insulating layer of warm air needs to be formed by placing another lightweight rug over the top of a sweat rug.

keeps the horse's loins warm. Make sure the sheet is pulled well up into the gullet of the saddle, to prevent it from putting pressure on the spine during exercise.

SUMMER SHEETS

These are usually made of cotton and are either used in the field during the summer to keep the sun off and flies away from the skin of a sensitive horse; when travelling, or just as a measure to keep dust off a stabled horse during the summer.

RUG FASTENINGS

Rollers

These are used to secure rugs where they do not have their own sewn-on straps, or where you have added under-blankets. They have a padded wither section which is often put on over a further foam pad to prevent localized pressure points. They run right around the horse's belly and should be accommodated

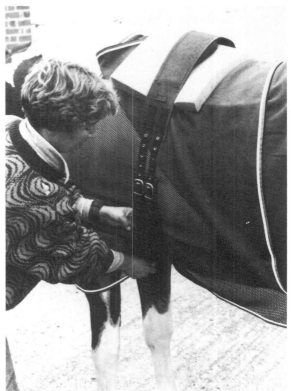

Always ensure that the rug is not wrinkled up under the roller.

146

Coolers are designed to take moisture away from the skin.

comfortably in the sternum curve (where the girth does up). They need to be done up firmly so that they prevent the rugs from slipping, but not as tight as a girth. Generally, you should be able to place the flat of your hand between the roller and the horse's sides.

Surcingles

These do the same job as a roller, but are not padded at the wither and are often not as wide. It is essential to use a wither pad with surcingles to prevent excessive pressure.

Cross-over Surcingles

These are sewn into the rugs, so you simply need to bring the rear strap on the off side to the front fixing point on the near side, and the front strap on the off side to the rear fixing point on the near side. In a correctly fitting rug these will cross over in the middle of the horse's belly.

Fillet Strings

These are used to prevent the rug from flying up over the back of the horse in windy conditions. They should be fitted fairly loosely under the tail but hang no lower than the end of the dock.

Leg Straps

These are usually found only on outdoor rugs, sometimes at both front and rear, but more commonly only at the rear. They should be linked through each other and fixed back on to the clip on their own side to provide extra stability and to prevent them from getting caught on the hocks. To prevent chafing you can slip fleece sleeves over them, or gel sleeves which are waterproof, but still soft.

ANTI-CAST ROLLER

As its name suggests, this helps to prevent the horse from becoming cast. It is a fairly hefty piece of equipment comprising a leather roller with padded wither sections to which a leather-covered metal loop is attached. The idea is that the horse cannot roll over while wearing one and cannot therefore get stuck

---
TACK TIP

While you may think a horse with white hairs over its withers has had a poorly fitting saddle, in truth many of these sores are caused by poorly fitting rollers, so take care when using them.

---

against the wall. In the main they are very suc-cessful at achieving their aim, but care does need to be taken with their use. In all cases a dense wither pad needs to be used under them, and doubly so if they are used without rugs, to prevent chafing and pressure sores.

ACCESSORIES

Hoods and Neck Covers

These are used as a means of controlling heat loss, or for preventing a horse from getting muddy while out in the field, although opinions vary as to the ethics of this – it is, after all, one of the horse's greatest pleasures! Perhaps they should be limited for use just prior to shows especially for grey horses. Some are simply hoods or neck covers which cover only the head or neck respectively, while others have neck cover and hood combined. Many rugs have matching neck covers and hoods, and if you need to use them then it is best to select these as they will have all the necessary fastenings.

If your rug does not have matching acces-sories, you can buy independent ones. Some

An anti-cast roller should have a dense pad under-neath it, especially if used without a rug under-neath, not as is shown here.

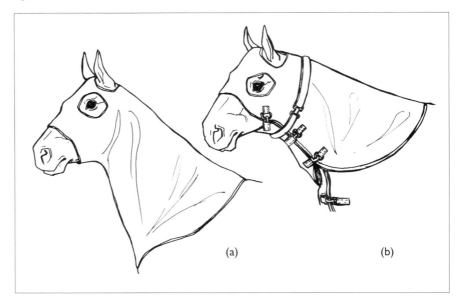

Types of hoods: (a) stretchy hood; (b) matching turnout hood and neck cover.

(a)   (b)

148

Anti-rubbing vest.

are loose fitting, simply draping over the neck and being secured by tapes or straps on the underside, while others are made of a light, stretchy material which is pulled on like a rubber glove. Many horses do not like the stretchy types of hood, so go carefully if you attempt to fit one to your horse.

Anti-Rubbing Vests

These are used under rugs to prevent them from rubbing bald patches at the shoulder, which is very common on horses living out full time. They are usually made of a stretch lycra fabric which is pulled on over the neck, with a roller sewn on to secure it just behind the withers. These are far more effective than sheepskin sewn into the chest of a rug.

Fly Veils

There are various different types of veil and fly fringe. Most are used to prevent flies from irritating sensitive horses while out at grass, but you will also see some horses wearing ones that completely cover the ears while competing indoors in order to prevent them from becoming overwhelmed by the noise.

A fly veil is used to prevent flies or noise irritating a sensitive horse.

149

12 Care and Maintenance

If you were to sit down and add up the cost of all the items of tack and equipment you have bought for your horse, you would probably be quite shocked by the results. Tack is necessary but it can also be expensive, so it is sensible to look after it properly. Well-cared-for tack will deter accidents, it will cost you less because it will last longer, and will prevent your horse from developing sores and injuries.

HOW TO CLEAN TACK AND EQUIPMENT

Tack which is used daily should be given a wipe over after each use and taken completely apart once a week so that you can check for signs of wear and tear and clean it thoroughly. To strip a bridle, undo all the buckles and take each piece apart, either lying them flat on a table or hanging them on a cleaning hook suspended from the ceiling. Place the bit into a bucket of clean warm water to soak. Put your saddle on a saddle horse, remove the girth and stirrup leathers and hang these up also. Remove the stirrup treads, and place these together with the irons in the bucket with the bit.

To clean the bridle and other lengths of leather such as the leathers and girth, firstly brush them over with a soft brush to remove any particles of grit or mud. Then wet a clean sponge and wring out all the excess water. Hang up each piece, one at a time. Wrap the sponge around the top of the piece and, while applying pressure, draw the sponge down to the bottom. Rinse the sponge and repeat until there is no grease or dirt left. It is acceptable to use tepid water, but do not use any kind of soap or detergent. If there are thick spots of grease (often known as jockeys because they stick like glue!) which prove difficult to remove, roll a few of your horse's tail hairs into a ball (usually obtainable from the brush you use when grooming) and rub the spots with this to shift them. If there is any grease or saddle soap caught in unused holes, use a matchstick, or opened paper-clip to push this out. Clean all the lengths of leather you have in this manner and then move on to the saddle. To clean a saddle, use a clean sponge as before, but rub in a circular motion until all the dirt and grease is removed. Use the ball of tail hair if necessary, paying particular attention to the underneath panels.

Clean off any dried saliva from the bit and any mud from the irons and treads with a nailbrush. You may need to use a household cleaner on white treads to bring them up really

TACK TIP

When undoing a bridle, make a note of the hole numbers, so that when you reassemble the bridle it will be the correct size for your horse. This will save time when bridling your horse and is a great advantage when bridling a horse which fidgets.

clean. Rinse in clean water and dry them thoroughly with a towel. Do not allow them to drip-dry as this encourages corrosion.

Once a saddle has been washed it will need to be treated with a leather preparation. What you decide to use will depend on the condition of your tack and the effectiveness of your routine care.

Always use a saddle soap containing glycerine.

Saddle Soap

Saddle soap is the traditional treatment for leather tack. It is not used to 'clean' tack in the way human soap is, but is designed to keep it supple and of a smart appearance. Soaps which contain glycerine are the best as these will condition the leather each time and keep it supple, removing the need for constant oiling. However, new advances are being made and we are now seeing leather care systems which do not use glycerine, but keep the tack in perfect order.

To apply saddle soap, always wet the soap not the sponge, as too much water will make the soap lather up which then makes it less effective and more difficult to apply. The seat of most saddles is made of a soft leather which usually stays relatively clean, so may only need a wipe over, but when soaping a saddle use wide circular movements. For lengths of leather, draw the sponge from top to bottom until a nice deep sheen is achieved and the leathers become pliable in your hands. Remember to push out any soap which has collected in the holes.

Some saddle soaps do stain, so make sure you choose one that does not or you might have to spend time cleaning your jodhpurs!

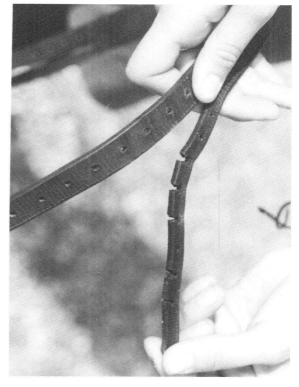

When taking tack apart, check for loose stitching or split leather. These split holes could cause a nasty accident: the item must *be replaced.*

Oiling

All tack needs oiling from time to time, but constant oiling of tack is unnecessary and can be damaging. New tack needs oiling more than used tack, and tack which has been drenched (perhaps in the rain or by being dunked at a water jump) will need regular oiling for a period of time until its suppleness returns.

Leather which has been regularly cared for with a glycerine saddle soap will only need to be oiled sparingly. If you oil your tack too much it will become limp and start to seep oil when bent. However, it is a good idea to apply a little oil in places where the tack regularly bends, such as the rein and bridle fastenings and the bend in the stirrup leathers, as this will prevent them from becoming brittle and cracking. Also remember that leather items which are continually getting wet, such as rug straps and leather boots, will need constant oiling to prevent them from chafing.

Some oils can rot the stitching, so use either pure neat's-foot oil or a special leather preparation of which there are many now available. To apply oil, simply stroke it on with a brush. Do not drench your tack, but if the leather does soak up the oil readily, apply another

coat and then oil it a few more times during the course of a week until it feels supple.

How to Care for Different Materials

Many saddle seats have an aniline, dyed finish which cannot be treated with ordinary saddle soaps or they end up resembling leopard skin. It is usual to use a wax-based product or cream for such saddles which should be applied in line with the manufacturer's instructions. If in doubt about your saddle seat, ask your saddler's advice.

Stirrup treads and other rubber items can be cleaned with ordinary household cleaners and a nail brush. Rinse and dry items thoroughly to ensure longevity.

Synthetic tack is very easy to clean and maintain. Bridles and saddles can simply be washed or even hosed, and some items can go in the washing machine.

Many pieces of equipment will be made of materials such as cotton or pure wool. To clean non-leather items, firstly remove any horse hairs and dirt with a brush. Many can then be put into the washing machine, but some may need to be hand washed, depending on the material. If washing by hand, use only a mild detergent as it is difficult to rinse the items thoroughly and any biological residues may irritate your horse's skin.

Some girths and numnahs can be put into the washing machine, but they may have buckles on. To prevent your machine from damage, put such items in a pillowcase before washing.

Having washed your equipment, pull items such as rugs and numnahs back into shape while still damp as some tend to 'crinkle' up while drying. Ensure all items are completely dry, which is best done by allowing them to hang in the sunshine, before re-use or storage. You can now buy 'rug' racks which allow rugs to be aired on a daily basis in the tack room. When not in use they fold back and lie flat against the wall.

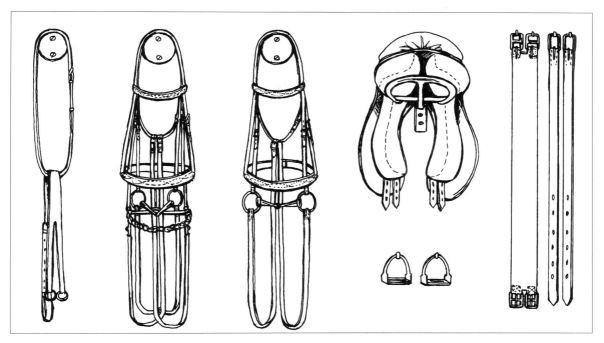

Correct storage of tack will ensure that it maintains its shape and will prevent damage.

Cleaning Bits and Metals

Bits simply need washing in clean water; they should never be polished with any form of metal polish. To shine a bit up, rub it with bran and then a soft clean cloth.

Other metal items can be polished with a metal polish. Most metal items of horse equipment are made of stainless steel which can be polished up well. Items such as buckles, which have movable parts, need extra care as they take a lot of pressure. After cleaning such items, apply a layer of grease to the tongues and joints once a week to keep them mobile and to prevent corrosion. This is also a sensible practice to adopt with bit-rings.

Brass-mounted bridles and headcollars will need polishing with a brass cleaner, but make sure you polish it off well, otherwise it leaves grey smears.

Be sure to remove all polish from around the tongues and links as if left, it will in time turn green and look horrible.

CORRECT STORAGE

Once items are clean and dry they need to be stored correctly or they will go out of shape or get damaged. To keep a bridle in good order, hang it on a semi-circular bracket. The throatlash can be used to hang the reins for everyday use, but after the weekly clean they look extra smart if they are passed through the throatlash, which is then assembled in a figure-of-eight design around the bridle.

Saddles should be put up fairly high on to saddle racks to ensure they do not get chewed by mice or knocked on to the floor. Cover them with a saddle cover or cotton sheet, but not polythene as this will encourage condensation, and thus mould, to form. All other lengths of leather should be hung by their buckles on hooks, away from the floor level. Other accessories, such as boots, should be put up on shelves. Rugs can either be suspended on high hooks, which allows them to air, or folded up and placed in trunks if only used occasionally.

Tack put up correctly will prevent both unnecessary damage and hours of searching for a lost item.

If you are not going to use any items for a long time they should be prepared for long-term storage. To store leather items, apply a thin layer of preservative to each, grease the buckles and wrap them in a cotton sheet. Place this in a trunk away from damp, mice and insects, preferably off the floor, and leave it in a secure, cool place.

Saddles should be treated in the same way but leave them on their racks, covered with permeable covers as leather sweats. Other non-leather items, once clean and dry, can be folded up and put into a trunk or a chest of drawers with moth balls or a strong scented soap (which also deters moths and other insects and vermin) for safe keeping. Also ensure any repairs are carried out before you put anything into storage, as you may need to use certain items unexpectedly, only to find they are broken.

> **— TACK TIP —**
>
> Before preparing tack and equipment for storage, give it a sponge down with a sterilizing wash to neutralize any infections which may be lurking. Tack which has been stored for some time may have a layer of mould on it. To clean this off, wash it with a sterilizing liquid before cleaning in the normal way. It is also a good idea to wipe any second-hand tack you may have bought with sterilizing fluid before use, to prevent the spread of any infections. **Warning**: do not use bleach of any kind as this will ruin your tack.

REPAIRS

If your horse has fallen while out riding, or you have accidentally dropped your saddle, have it checked by a saddler for damage to the tree. A broken saddle tree means a useless saddle; it cannot, or at least should not, be

154

repaired. To check for a broken tree, try pushing on either side of the front arch, and if you can feel excessive movement be wary – have it checked by your saddler. Similarly, hold the pommel on your hip and try to move the cantle up and down – excessive movement means a likely broken tree.

As a safety precaution it is a good idea to have all tack checked annually by your saddler. However, you may notice minor defects in between times which need seeing to immediately. Common areas of weakness include:

Stitching
Stitching can work loose or start to rot and unless you inspect it regularly you may not notice any flaws until it is too late. Pay particular attention to areas which take a lot of strain, such as leathers, the girth and reins.

Saddle flocking
This often becomes flat or lumpy and, again, unless you look for it you might not notice any difference. Flat or lumpy flocking will cause saddle sores so have your saddler reflock and then refit your saddle at the first signs of trouble. New flocking settles after a few weeks, so make sure your saddle still fits after this time.

Metal parts
Bit-rings and joints can become loose and rough with wear, and will pinch your horse's mouth. If this happens to your bit, it is worn out so you need to invest in a new one. Bits are not repairable.

While bits and saddle trees are irreparable, there are simple repairs which you can safely undertake yourself.

To Repair Stitching on Leather

1. You will firstly need to acquire some saddlery needles and waxed linen thread of the right colour. Your saddler will happily supply these or you can use ordinary blunt-ended darning-type needles and plaiting thread coated in beeswax which helps to prevent it from wear and rotting due to horse sweat, rain and rubbing.
2. Next remove all the old stitching with a pair of tweezers.
3. Take a piece of thread no longer than 60cm (24in) and thread a needle on to each end of it.
4. If the piece you are restitching has a buckle attached, make sure this is the correct way around before you begin. Check the buckle first as you may be better off replacing this as well rather than re-using the old one.
5. Insert one of the needles through the first vacant hole and pull it through until you have an equal length of thread on either side of the leather. Hold the piece of leather out in front of you and, starting with the needle on your left, push it through the next hole from left to right. Then push your right-hand needle through the same hole from right to left. Pull the thread taut on either side so that the leather draws together. The needles have exchanged places and you have a stitch on both the top and bottom of the leather. Make another stitch over the top of these for added strength then work along the length of the leather in the same fashion, towards the point where the stitching is once again sound or to the end hole if you are stitching a whole new row.
6. Go back over the last two stitches so that they are double-stitched for strength.
7. After completion of the last stitch, push the right-hand needle back though the previous hole, so that you end up with both needles on the underside.
8. Cut the threads so that they lie flush with the leather.
9. Lay the item on a flat surface and gently tap the stitches with a wide-faced hammer to flatten and lay them. This will prevent them from being rubbed or worked loose.
10. Repeat the process for each row of stitching. Remember that stirrup leathers may have three rows so make sure you do them all.

MAINTENANCE AND CLEANING OF RUGS

All rugs should be hung up in a cool dry place when not in use. Many modern rugs can simply be put into an industrial washing machine (your household one will be too small) and then hung up to dry naturally. However, check that the fittings are also suitable for washing in a machine before doing so. Synthetic rugs will often need to have their seams resealed to prevent water from entering along the stitches. Canvas rugs will need reproofing at least once through the winter and possibly two or three times, depending on the fabric and reproofer used. You should use the reproofer stated in the manufacturer's instructions, or in the absence of such instructions ask your retailer to recommend a suitable one. Also remember that straps, fittings and stitching should be checked and cleaned regularly. Leather items will need to have a suitable dressing or oil applied on a regular basis to maintain their suppleness and strength. Metal fittings should have a little oil applied at the same time to keep them pliable.

TACK TIP

Having purchased a new rug, do not throw your old one out as it will come in handy as a spare when you need to reproof, clean, dry or repair the newer one.

To Repair Rugs

Many rugs are made of materials that can simply be stitched up if torn; however, this does not apply so easily to traditional New Zealand rugs, as the canvas is heavy duty and waterproofed. Due to their constant use, and the environment in which they are used, New Zealand rugs are often torn on fence posts or trees. If you repair a small rip immediately you notice it, you can prevent a larger tear from appearing. To repair a traditional canvas-type New Zealand rug, all you need is a canvas patch and a pot of latex glue (Copydex

is excellent for this job as it is waterproof). Cover the patch and the underside of the rug with glue and simply sandwich together. Place a small board over the patch and stand on it until it has all bound together and the glue has moulded itself into the contours of the fabric. If the New Zealand is a waxed cotton type, simply reapply a layer of wax reproofing agent which can be obtained from any saddler's or camping shop.

The buckles on rugs are another item which often give way during constant use. Metal buckles which give will need to be completely replaced. If attached to a leather rug strap this will mean removing the stitching, replacing the old buckle with a new one and then stitching back up as described for leather. However, if you have to do this you might consider changing the leather straps for nylon web, as these last longer and can be washed. You might also consider changing the metal buckle for a nylon clip fastener if appropriate for the job. These are often seen on modern rugs, as they simply push together and can be put into the washing machine without damage. These, too, are readily available from camping shops.

PREVENTING TACK THEFT

Tack theft seems to be a popular pastime for thieves, so it makes sense to invest in some security measures to safeguard your equipment. Firstly, you must do all you can to prevent thieves from taking your tack in the first place, but should this happen you also need to be able to identify the tack as yours.

Methods of Prevention

To protect tack from theft you can now buy various anti-theft devices, such as specially designed saddle-safe gadgets, lockable tack racks, trunks and cabinets which fix to the wall.

The saddle safe consists of galvanized steel cable, formed into a T-shape with each end

A method of identifying tack using metal identity punches. Most people stamp on their post code or date of birth to avoid disputes over ownership.

It is often said that nothing will stop a determined thief and certainly if they come prepared with bolt cutters then they intend to take everything they can lay their hands on. Lockable tack racks are good, in that a metal frame comes down over the top of the saddle and physically prevents the saddle from being lifted off the rack. However, they can mark your saddle if you have a soft leather seat and cantle, so always ensure your saddle is covered before putting it on the rack and make sure the frame sits snugly on your saddle. If any movement is allowed, thieves will try to pull it free and while they may not succeed, they may cause a lot of damage to your saddle in the process. In one recent case of theft where a tack room was burgled, all that was left were two saddles protected by these racks, so they do work as a deterrent.

Lockable trunks and cabinets are also a good idea as long as they are well fixed down. In all cases, where there are both unprotected and protected items of tack, the unprotected ones have been stolen. Anything which is going to delay thieves or cause them to make a noise while they know the police could be on their way, acts as a good preventative.

Methods of Identification

Should the worst happen and, despite your vigilance, your tack gets stolen, you need to be able to identify it as your own should it be recovered. There are various ways of doing this, including using metal identity punches, photographs, indelible labelling and by inserting a special identifying tag just inside the saddle flocking which can be read by an automatic scanning device. While employing such measures, also make a comprehensive inventory of your tack, with serial numbers and any special distinguishing marks listed by each item. Such measures will prove ownership and they will also help in proving the value of your tack for an insurance claim.

terminating in a loop. Once the saddle is returned to a standard saddle rack after use, it can simply and quickly be locked into place, preventing unlawful removal. The gadget is fitted over the saddle and the three end loops of the T shape are secured with a padlock to the cross member of the saddle rack. The cables are covered in padded webbing to prevent any damage to the saddle, and it is impossible to remove the saddle from the rack without actually cutting through the cable with bolt cutters, or physically pulling the whole saddle rack and saddle from the wall. It would certainly deter opportunist thieves, or other members of a livery yard from practising that most annoying habit of 'borrowing' your tack without permission.

Index